And Then the Vulture Eats You

And Then the Vulture Eats You

*True Tales About Ultramarathons
and Those Who Run Them*

Edited by John L. Parker, Jr.
Author of *Once a Runner* and *Again to Carthage*

BREAKAWAY BOOKS
HALCOTTSVILLE, NEW YORK
2011

Originally published by Cedarwinds Publishing Company.

Current edition published by
Breakaway Books
P.O. Box 24
Halcottsville, NY 12438
www.breakawaybooks.com

Front cover art by John L. Parker, Jr.

Library of Congress Cataloging in Publication Data

Parker, Jr., John L. (Ed.) 1947-   And Then the Vulture Eats You.

1. Runners (Sports)—Biography—Addresses, essays, lectures. 2. Running races—Addresses, essays, lectures. 3. Running—Marathons. I. Title
GV1061.16.P66   796.4'26 [B]

10   9   8   7   6   5   4   3   2   1

Contents

Thanks . . .

. . . to Peter Gagarin, Stan Wagon, and Dan Brannen, all of *Ultrarunning*, for early guidance.

. . . to the late Karen Girard, for years of friendship as well as stalwart assistance in the editorial trenches.

. . . to my longtime friend Meg Waldron, for a great, late suggestion.

. . . to Don Kardong, not only for his fine writing, but also for his wonderfully graphic line about a vulture, a line which I shamelessly appropriated and which became the title for this book.

This book is for Jack Bacheler, father of the Florida Track Club, my mentor and friend, who taught the rest of us how to run.

—J.L.P

Introduction

What manner of beast lurks in the sweaty ethers out there beyond the 26.2 mile post? What manner of rare enkephalin does your brain secrete in reward or dismay? And now that we've had any number of great grandmoms happily finish marathons, where, finally, are the *real* limits to what the human animal can persuade itself to endure on foot?

The writers in this book have done their best to find out some pretty difficult things and have come back to tell you about them. It cost most of them.

The only other thing I have to add by way of introduction is to mention that running my fingers lightly over the handiwork of these writers has been just about my happiest experience as an editor.

There wasn't much, honestly, to do, except occasionally shake my head and cluck, "Oh my, now *that* was certainly deft."

—John L. Parker, Jr.

P.S. The term "ultramarathon," the conceptual umbrella for this volume, is admittedly used rather loosely. Purists among the Ultranauts will probably insist that a true ultramarathon is a *continuous* footrace longer than a marathon. However, in searching for the highest quality material I could find for this volume, it became useful to also include stage races, multi-race events, and even one informal solo marathon-plus effort.

To those thus offended, I can only beg your indulgence. As a former miler with all of three marathons to his credit, I have to admit that I look upon ultras the same way I do mountain-climbing, which is to say with macabre fascination. It's all madness to me.

SWIFTS ON THE WING

James E. Shapiro

Seventeen of us line up, fresh as un-wrinkled peas, about to be sent whirling off by a gun's crack, circling round and round a 400-meter track, caught in a dream of our own choosing—a nightmare some might call it—because for the next 144 hours we would have nothing to do but devote ourselves to staying in motion as long as we could.

It was early November 1981 and for the first time since 1903 a six-day track race was being held on English soil. Like 19th-century endurance prototypes so wildly popular in the Victorian era, this event too was of the "go-as-you-please" variety. There really is no other way to run them; you must be able to run and walk for as long as you want and come off the track at will for periods of rest, eating, sleeping and massage.

Most of us would be on the track 16 to 18 hours a day. Some would sleep in a trackside tent that swarmed with activity; others like myself would dash off to nearby hotels for a few hours of troubled sleep, tormented by burning feet, sore joints and overtired bodies. Some runners would say much later, when we emerged on the other side of this trial, that they didn't dream about the race while it was actually on but that they did during the first free night.

Certainly there was no way to escape the feverish intoxication of the race. Only once during those six days and nights did the number of competitors sink to just one. At every moment somebody or some bodies moved round the track, ceaselessly at work, so that no matter when you slept, the relentless advance of your competitors seeped through the chill night air, made you awaken with that sobering sense that not another instant could be wasted. It was like war.

You can't go through something like that halfway and you don't really go through it alone. We'd be on a short piece of track in a community of other runners, all sharing just one thing in common: fascination with distance. Going through it, too, in their own way would be the trackside officials, lap-counters, local townsfolk, wives, handlers, relatives, as well as the fellow in the electric wheelchair out every morning saying "Come on, lads!" And finally there were the odd souls, at first moved by simple curiosity and then increasingly fascinated, who were irrevocably drawn back night after night, coming straight from their jobs, as their friendships with specific runners intensified.

But we could not have guessed any of this at ten minutes before the start at the Harvey Hadden Stadium in Nottingham, England on a bright November afternoon. Such sweetness and release can only taste the way they do after one deserves them. This temporary community had not yet begun to establish itself.

Most of us had never run a six-day race, so the start was about as constrained and undramatic as I have ever seen for an ultramarathon. There was a modest shuffling about in the front ranks just in back of the starting stripe. No one wanted to take the inside front spot, so with a self-conscious determination I took it. It was hard to read the mood of the others; not until there were literally a handful of seconds left did everyone come out of hiding to take their places for a 144-hour race that could become more than 500 miles long by its finish.

At the gun, the bunch of us creaked into motion. A breeze drove leaves against the fence around our pit-like enclosure. The track, a faded brown underfoot, was bounded on each side by the high, banked walls of a bicycle-racing track. The grass on the infield was green. Overhead were patches of blue, a rarity in England.

This was it, the great beginning that commenced as all ultras must, with the squirreling away of inches, feet, yards, a handful of miles until much later someone would end the dream and tell you how far you went. The plucked yellow branches of a stand of poplars gleamed in the bright sunshine. The 17 of us ran on, wedded to the track and to one another for what might as well have been forever.

Wobbles

We have a long way to travel, in a literal sense, to match the accomplishments of the golden era of six-day races, which flourished in the late 1800s. In the 20-year period before the turn of the century the best ultra-pedestrians or "peds" (such as Edward P. Weston who clocked 500 miles around a New Jersey rink in 1874) were international sports heroes replete with prize money and glory. A lively rivalry between England and America sprang up as contestants criss-crossed the Atlantic. (In a mild echo of that, one of the English spectators would wring my hand at the end of the Nottingham race saying, "Well done . . . for a Colonial!")

Six-day road runs began at least as early as the 1770s during an age when lords relied upon their footmen as couriers, since running great distances was the best means of communication then. Well on into the 19th century the tradition of titled patrons subsidizing such men continued, for much the same reason that some men revel in the possession of a fast horse. During the Victorian era, it was a sport that drew primarily from the working class and offered a chance for the bold and hardy to win plaudits from the aristocracy that graced the crowds of spectators.

The popular name for such events, "the wobbles," described both the peculiarity of a classical walker's gait as well as the tottering style those in terminal exhaustion exhibited. The phrase "go-as-you-please" referred to the mix of mongrel walking and running styles. But why six days? A more pious age than our own frowned upon athletic competition on Sundays. So wobbles usually started late on a Sunday night and finished before midnight the following Saturday.

Just as it took the Victorian peds a good 15 years of challenging their limitations before expanding their capacities, so it will probably require some years for our own modern crew of ultra fanatics to push their limits out, slowly. Only experience teaches one all the manifold pitfalls of an ultra; developing a feel for judging effort in such a concentrated endeavor takes practice. One could compare the six-day race to an equation, a problem, a dilemma that has only one answer—to go forward, working with all one's might and all one's cunning. The race we set out to do that Nottingham November in 1981 was the kind that goes to those who judge their limits with precision.

"I like to think of it this way," said Mike Newton of the South London Harriers, a heavy pre-race favorite, "that my body is given out to me on loan and I have to return it at the end of the day. So you can't bash it to bits, can you, when you've got to get up the next day and start all over again."

Anyone able to run 80 to 85 miles a day could fancy himself a likely winner. Everyone was expected to be easily capable of doing 250 miles, the minimum amount required for a trophy. Not that another piece of plastic-and-marble twaddle with some third-rate figurine of an ersatz gold runner meant much, but it did draw the line in the sand. No one had really committed himself to any prediction in the Nottingham race but there were a few runners there who surely were thinking of 500 and beyond. Joe Record, the big-jawed Australian, confided later in the race that he had been aiming for 600 miles. I had said to myself, I'll shoot for something in the high 400s but settle for 500!

Day One

1.	Choi	115.57 miles
2.	Newton	111.34
3.	Record	110.10
4.	Towers	103.14

5.	Campbell	101.65
6.	Harney	95.93
7.	Collins	95.69
8.	Shapiro	94.44
9.	Morris	91.71
10.	Dixon	91.21

Handlers

On the second day of the race it looked like the whole thing might come unraveled, though by the third day organizational problems began to be solved. Ultra runners are sometimes surprisingly daffy about practical matters. Only four of us had come with a full-time handler. A handler is not a necessity for a race but he or she can make a considerable difference. Eventually someone has to carry weight for you if you can't do it yourself. A dozen extra steps becomes a tremendous aggravation when you are pushing your edge out hour after hour.

The type of help provided by modern handlers is particularly appreciated when you consider the practices of old. The handlers of those long-ago heroes of the ultra were quick to employ methods of rejuvenation that would be considered appalling nowadays. They included doses of belladonna, strychnine, electric shocks and, in one famous case, the application of a 16-bladed scarificator to a runner's thighs. The multi-bladed knives cut an eighth inch deep into the runner's skin in the hopeful belief that bleeding would relieve muscle soreness and fatigue. In fact, the man went on to win his race.

Fortunately the handlers at our race in Nottingham were less experimental, but just as devoted. Mike Newton's parents manned an aid station on the far stretch. They stood there for hours, patiently refilling squeeze bottles with the drinks he wanted, watching and waiting, double-checking their counts of his laps with those of the timekeepers. Mike's parents carried his gear out to the taxi when they left for meals or a night's sleep.

John Towers's wife was another patient soul who was there as long as John was. In the latter stages of the race when his knees and ankles were giving him tremendous pain, she would quietly urge him to go easy. He never seemed to take her advice but in the mysterious ways of couples he seemed to retreat from the boiling edge of emotional outbreak after such talks. Paul Collins was also closely watched over by his wife Betty. I had my close friend Donna Hudson as handler.

The handler is thrown into an intimate relationship with the runner. And that holds true whether or not your handler is a man as they all were in the old days. This is a physical sport about bodies and pain and tension. It's got to do with loyalties and knowing when to say no and when to take advice. Your feet get massaged, your clothing gets washed, your bath gets run, your meals cooked, drinks set out, wet rain gear changed for dry, the position of the enemy is whispered into your ears alone. Your state of mind in all its changes from steady workaday sobriety through depression and nastiness is shared, as is that hug you need when you think you just can't go on without a human embrace because your joints are on fire. Going through all that, the handler's loyalty is tremendous.

Donna, whose temper can be as red as her hair, was in a state of simmering outrage about the organizational flaws by the second day. Because the digital clock had broken, Laps were being timed by a wristwatch with only a sweep second hand; on top of that, the timers' tent was unheated. The only food supplies the sole volunteer in the kitchen had were milk, bread, eggs and dried pasta. Day or night, any time a famished runner came up for a meal, the fare seemed to be scrambled eggs and toast. No one thought to take hot coffee or tea down to the chilled trackside officials and volunteers. Volunteers themselves began to dwindle in alarming numbers. It was all getting stretched thin, as were the tempers of many people there.

So it was hardly surprising when Donna and one of the organizers got into a loud and bitter altercation on the stadium steps that second day. Not only Donna but Betty Collins as well had been worn ragged by taking on chores for other runners who seemed sorely in need of them. The two organizers Bob Holmes and Geoff Richardson were both in the race, so naturally they were defensive and irritated by the criticism. It was a sticky, complicated business. But in that tiny community we had to get along, and it would have been unbearable to maintain a silent feud for the next 100 hours.

Conditions improved dramatically when the Nottingham Building Society, a major sponsor, brought heated tents and trailers to the track, rushed in supplies of fresh vegetables and otherwise improved things.

Day Two

1.	Record	202.06 miles
2.	Newton	193.37
3.	Harney	162.79
4.	Campbell	162.30
5.	Morris	161.05
6.	Shapiro	157.82
7.	Dixon	157.08
8.	Towers	156.58
9.	Choi	150.86
10.	Parsons	134.96

Children's Brigade

The ones who really saved the six-day, though, were the juveniles who seeped in from the local neighborhood. Eleven to 18 years of age, these brash, spunky kids worked hard, mostly as lap recorders. One of the serious crew-cut heads bent over the lap sheets calling out "Got you, number 17 . . ." belonged to an older boy who had been in some rough business, stolen a few dozen cars and taken six inches of knife blade into his stomach in a fight; he was, he said, ready for a quieter life.

When I was a Peace Corps volunteer in a rural Brazilian town, I discovered the phenomenon of *cabras* or "goats"—young lads who would attach themselves to you with instinctive, unquestioning loyalty and follow you everywhere. In Nottingham my own *cabra* was Philip, a 15-year-old kid with a narrow face and a lanky frame, usually dressed despite the chill in black pants and a thin black zip-up windbreaker. He counted laps, repaired the generator when it went on the fritz and periodically ran up to me with a ragged slip of paper on which he had scrawled the relative positions of my nearest rivals.

After the race was over I gave him some of the shirts and rain gear given me by the sponsors. An hour later as I sat eating hors d'oeuvres in the clubhouse, an officious adult hauled Philip back with a firm grip.

"This chap claims you gave him these things. . . ." Philip's dark eyes looked sad. It was better just to be simple so I said, yes, it was fine.

"Well, you never know . . ." the older man said. I couldn't help but wonder whether he would have been so distrusted had he been wearing a tie and blazer.

Then there were the schoolchildren. They came every morning around 8:00 or 8:30, chattering on the other side of the fence like sparrows. The bolder ones clambered over to join us, especially excited about demonstrating to their friends how they were entering the precincts of the adult world. Even the most jaded of us perked up, for, worn down as we were, we could not resist those bright eyes and rosy complexions and that shrill patter of questions.

"Ey, Mister, ain't cha feelin' tired now?"

Oh, god, from what gray depths we could answer that, but the question was simple enough, and explaining was easier because children don't ask why.

"Oh, yes, I'm a little tired."

"What time did you go to sleep then?"

"Midnight."

"Oh! And what time did you start again?"

"At seven this morning."

"And you'll be running all day while I'm in school until I come back again, ey ?"

"That's right."

"I told my mum about you. I told her I ran two laps with you."

I looked down at the eleven-year-old who himself ran in school, at the two little sisters who scrambled along, school satchels banging on their legs, red cheeks glowing in the middle of their neat, brushed-up features. Suddenly drawn by the call of school, they vanished, chattering madly as they took flight. The track fell quiet again or quiet in the special way that the generator thudding away made it sound, the quiet of a factory or a dockyard. We were running alone then, having to do for ourselves what no one else could, adults beating our brains out for obscure reasons.

Morning was not the most sociable part of the day in our world, the day stretching out with no foreseeable surprises, not close to lunch, too bright for sleeping; no reason at all for a break. By now, familiar enough with each other, we could tell by the sound who was coming up behind, yet the almost automatic cheering-on kind of comment we so constantly doled out to one another was, by common and unspoken consent, withheld for a while. Slaves on the galley sometimes take more comfort in their work than in the nearness of others who share their bench.

It was a time for private observations. A flock of geese sassed across the great bowl of sky overhead heading south. Television cameramen holding cups of steaming tea in their hands cast curious glances at us as we trotted past. The timekeeper kept to his chanting of the time, the lap-scorers raised their gloved hands to tell passing runners that, yes, they had seen them and were entering this latest piece of work in the ledger.

It would be a gray world for two hours, a world of work while you backed off from the mental calculations because they couldn't soften your mood; hard to say where such hours went or what they felt like. They felt like sensation, like arms moving, chilly wind making part of your face feel alive as you rounded the bend; hours like houses coming into view, then vanishing, leaving trees again, now the signboard, and then the growing awareness of the tongue that signals thirst, the discussion in the mind of when to get a drink and what kind of drink to get and whether it should be sugared or not, and all the while the world continued to slither through and you slid into the world so the hours didn't bring boredom to contend with, rather they brought difficulties that sought attention then faded only to return again.

Different parts of the body chafed, burned, begged in some way or another for release; so many needs—for toilet, food, sleep, even for friendliness. These demands didn't so much interrupt the work as become part of the work. The sacredness of these small preoccupations, miraculously, was understood by others.

"Do you need more ice for your foot?" someone asked me when I was lying on my back in the main tent with my bare feet tilted askew on a chair. Ice meant release from pain, the chance to work again, the chance to nurse my hurting way along a bit farther. Ice—it was almost an embodiment of the impersonal respect others bore us for the effort. None of the helpers, old hands after three days, ever asked "why are you doing it?" The journalists asked it, the first-timers asked it, but everyone else took it for granted that it was important to work.

One small bird-like woman ran with me for a while. She was full of talk about swifts, an ubiquitous bird in England. "You know they are always in flight," she said. "They mate on the wing, sleep on the wing, eat on the wing—do everything while they fly, even give birth that way. I heard of a swift that fell down a chimney, and when they examined it they found it was 17 years old. It was the first time in its life it had probably ever been on the ground."

The funny thing was she could not know how strangely stirring it was to hear all that. We, too, were temporarily like swifts, doomed to prodigious effort.

"You feel as if you want to help the runners achieve their goals," she said. Then she went on to say something that was so clear, so illuminating that I thought I would not forget the exact way she phrased it, but now that has faded beyond recall. It was something of an expression of wondering that people like herself, who came along to run with the runners, to bear them a little company and cheer, people who worked without pay such long hours doing such seemingly mundane things as counting laps, became so caught up in it.

"Why?" I asked.

"Because you become part of their effort," she said, which to me meant we become you and you become us, and there is no better feeling than that.

Day Three

1. Newton 283.59 miles
2. Record 267.43
3. Campbell 224.43
4. Harney 221.95
5. Morris 220.46

Friends and Enemies

We began to look older. By the fourth and fifth days most of us were out to 300, 400 miles and the strain was clear. Hook lines near the bottom of the nose slanted down past the mouth on unshaven faces; I felt a softening of boundaries between myself and other people.

On the fifth day I came up behind Malcom Campbell, both of us trotting with great concentration, and after the usual pleasantries I asked, "Where are you in mileage?" and was surprised at myself. Never before had Malcom and I mentioned the delicate issue of how much we monitor one another. He paused, smiled, answered however many miles it was, and to signal appreciation of his candor, I said, "You're a tough one to bury, Malcom. I keep waiting for you to drop off. You're really an inconsiderate bastard." We laughed over that kind of thing for a few moments and, linked now by our confession to a sense of common cause against those in front of us, we discussed our chances relative to the leaders.

"If they crack," he confided, his ruddy complexion glowing beneath his carefully brushed silver thatch, "then we have a chance to come up through the ranks." He was being polite. He would not wait for me nor I for him. So this was a charged confidentiality tinged with bad-boy secrets. My foot felt terrible and I was hoping Malcom would hit one of his exhausted stages soon. I said nothing about my foot, he nothing of his own worries, but we parted better friends than before, each knowing that the other was not meant to know all.

Gerald Parsons had a maddened, owlish glow some hours, during one of which we tried to talk to him. "Don't bother me," he said. "I'm getting close to 300 now. Must concentrate." We knew what it meant to be steaming full throttle for some port with a couple of zeros in its name, so we said not a word more.

Tall Colin Dixon, whose good humor rarely seemed to desert him, was another shark waiting to gobble me up as I began to lose ground. One evening in the tent I was waiting for the doctor while Colin was being examined first. Glancing down I saw his lower left shin, violently colored as if he had dipped it into a tub of pitch hot water. He has big feet like mine and, looking down at all the purply red splendor, I felt a kind of grim joy at the enemy being hobbled, sorrow for a companion's troubles and an abashed sense that he was taking a steady beating, too, without his showing any movement of the face except a wry grin.

Campbell fell asleep in the tub twice in the last few days, awoke badly chilled and stiff. He would plod on for a few hours in sodden misery. Joe Record had to switch to different shoes for his feet. Mike Newton retired early on the fifth day because he couldn't breathe properly and, on the sixth, confessed to swollen ankles. John Towers's knees and ankles were so badly swollen, he was constantly icing them down. Such was the price for such nonsense.

Once Don Choi was hobbled by blisters, the race for first spot came down to a battle between Joe Record and Mike Newton. The two of them stalked each other like cats. At one memorable moment, much the way bidders in an auction hall give a steady gaze of appraisal to the one shadow lying between them and victory, Mike and Joe looked clearly at each other, the head of each swiveling to get a fix on his opponent. For a while it was not a jot different than the ego-breaking tactics favored by the Victorian peds. It had always seemed moderately insane to care whether an opponent passed you once in a while during a race many hundreds of miles long. Yet I found in this race an astonishing tendency, exemplified by myself as well as by Mike and Joe, to fixate on one's rivals.

The yellow rain top of the man down the track did not simply enter my eye, wash through my mind and out again; rather it was seized upon by an anxious ego and called an enemy, its position remembered, its place on the charts recalled. Everything in the six-day hammered at me to defend my position.

Every two to two-and-a-half minutes I passed the timers' tent, heard my time called, heard other times called; 25 times an hour I passed the boards with the other names scrawled upon them. It was hard to get free the way I could alone on the roads when no one was judging my distance and no one was saying I should be faster or slower. It was hard to keep waking into the moment, free of the demons of past and future, when I was always being jostled by a literal-minded set of men and women, their minds besotted with numbers that told you where you had been and, hence, where you were bound for. It was too hard to let go, to leave it alone, and the price for me of such subliminal, unrecognized tension was a self-intoxicating weariness.

Day Four

1.	Newton	352.68 miles
2.	Record	328.58
3.	Harney	300.49
4.	Campbell	279.61

Under the Big Top

The big tent became the village common, the floating community, the tribal lodge house in which everything was tended to within a few square feet. I particularly remember one night, don't know any more which it was, maybe the last. I lay on my back with legs up on a chair, a plastic bag of melting ice draped over my ankle, a wool cap pulled down to my eyebrows, arms resting on my chest. Such a simple thing: the way your arms fold and the warmth and pressure of them. They were on vacation, not obliged to move. A rest in this tired space seemed like a sweet little meadow way up on the snowy heights of this mountain I was trying to scale.

I remember looking up at the yellow skin of the tent overhead, at the delicacy with which the lines of its rippled surface fanned away from the center pole. The wind made the tent shake and flap, but all that tumult outside rendered the warmth inside even more snug. Twenty voices chattered—as if spinning a radio dial, I could pick out one band of energy at a time—one was the timer, a small lad with a big mouth and a nasal British accent massacring his "aitches," his "twenty-two-oh-six!" fervent and loud as a work master's chant.

The runners staggered in out of the night, seamen lashed by the sea. They groaned, slumped into chairs, grimly lowered themselves to the floor, crawled inside sleeping bags, closed their eyes to sleep, able like the devil's children to forget immediately if briefly the labor that awaited them.

In one corner of the tent, microwave ovens cooked frozen pizza and shepherd's pies. A photographer knelt near by, snapping away as a trainer massaged a runner's white legs. At the front of the tent lap-counters sat blowing on their hands, squinting under the bright arc lights. Extras, men and women, some familiar, some not, stood, watching the way so many watch, with the barefaced interest of those who are drawn by the spectacle of apparitions emerging out of the night. Why did they wait and watch? How different could each runner look in the space of 20 minutes? There was nothing special about their speed, their muscularity. They offered no witty sallies at this hour, but they did communicate a profound sense of commitment and repose, a kind of peacefulness of purpose in their silence, under all the noise and the dud-dud-dud thudding of the generator. Our tent lights burned long after more formal family households dropped off to sleep.

Nottingham slept but we went on. After the witching hour was when you really knew you were down to the hardcore zanies, in with a special crew on that track, as alone now as you could ever be on this great planet, looking up at the clouds passing over the face of the moon. Their centers were dark but luminescent on the edges where a cloud is thinnest. The moon that last night came up early, rose right out of a distant sidewalk, a great perfect orange wafer so enormous that the other runners' voices cracked with glee in welcoming it. As it rose it grew steelier and paler and with each quarter, smaller. Far below tiny men continued on their own, endlessly circular way. It got cold at such hours so all you could do was zip up your parka, sling your hands in your pockets and stump along, heedless of everything except going on without hope, without resentment, without desire.

Everyone was strung out, just a few beads on a string. The loudspeakers were quiet but back at the tent some appreciative hand-clapping from the few lap-counters, kids really, young Lords of the night, who were shouting at those trotting past. "Number 17 coming up! Fifty-four dead . . . fantastic, lad! . . . great going . . . keep going!"

They hugged us in this fashion every time we came round. I started to *want* to come round, to please them, to please myself. Then, with the tent behind me, while with me were the long cold backstretch, the damp wind, the wasted winter whiteness of the moon, strange thoughts would visit, the hoping that everyone else would die off and just I alone were winning, the ultimate competitive fantasy. But after an hour, fantasy always fell away, leaving the sore legs, the grinding need for a drink, the foggy bad patch where I got down on my mental knees and started counting minutes, talking myself through, fighting the urge to quit, to give in to the desire to sit down, to do something *human*. But that wasn't what the six days were about. So I'd compromise and stop for tea, grinning at the simple pleasures life could offer, hot tea steaming between my mittened hands and the feel of the ground under my feet

Day Five

1.	Newton	426.5 miles
2.	Record	385.49
3.	Harney	365.86
3.	Morris	365.86
4.	Campbell	346.72

The Last Morning

Here we were, just as we had to be, finding ourselves alive and moving on the last day of the race. Little details, gritty problems— planning how to get home, packing one's gear—all these anticipatory details began to seep into the coloration of our minds. We were getting ready to become civilians again. By late morning a crowd began to fill the stands.

One thing hasn't changed in the hundred years since six-day races were at their zenith—those who run them suffer. In the abuse of the flesh was direct evidence of determination.

Dave Hayward, 29 then and a brigade fireman, ran with his eyes closed for long stretches and carried his elongated frame with a sense of compression too, as if engaged in a battle with fear. He seemed to be in a perpetual state of wincing, as if waiting for the idea of all that distance and time to crush him. Yet on that last day, he nearly covered 100 miles, loping past, elbows working, his pale complexion flushed, the hissing sound of his breathing communicating an excitement, a growing joy and a certainty that *yes*, he was rallying. To go so long, to reach down so deep and find it possible after all, almost easy in a way, with each successive lap—that's the feeling that kept igniting the jaded carbon heap of body into fresh fire.

Malcom Campbell's style for confronting disintegration was effective. Those of us who awaited his downfall were always disappointed. With his hefty body and ample waist, Malcom ran in badly pronated style and altogether looked like a jogger you could catch up with and surpass. He was certainly passable at times but at others, particularly when his favorite Elton John tune came over the loudspeakers, he dashed around the track at a tremendous clip, his pink face lit and glowing. Periodically, he'd vanish for an hour's hot tub, and then, awash in energy and hopefulness, he'd be spinning around at a tremendous clip again.

"I think I'm a bit of a survivor," Malcom said later in a species of British understatement.

By the last day, it was an exalted yet punchy little wartime camp. The end of the long march was in sight. So much had happened, so many endless postings of positions, so many broken hours of sleep where waking up each time made it seem like a whole other day, so much a sense of having lived a month in a few hours. Yesterday? That was an infinity away.

Joe Record broke out a bottle of sherry he had conjured up from somewhere and now in the last hours, as his own second-place position seemed fairly well assured, he shifted into increasingly manic moments of sociability. Word went round about the miracle of sherry. Just a few nips of the warm liquid made the body glow.

Later Joe waxed philosophical about how it felt to run this long. "It's a mode of living in which energies flow and I learn and I'm aware. They say, What do you think about? But thoughts cycle.

31

They're boring and the mind comes to a stop here and there, or thoughts are spacing out and I'm getting a very bright retinal discharge like an acid trip. Sometimes you feel really bad, and then suddenly it's quite pleasant really. All these energies that come from going right through the night, day after day like that!

"It was nice encountering those school kids. The first couple of days they're a little puzzled. They soon find out they love you and introduce you to the other kids. You run all night and you'll be there in the morning for them. As they got to know me, I got to know them. I'm a 40-year-old adult and I don't have any children of my own. As you get older you seem to lose your ability to love— suddenly here it is the same as it's always been—open and vulnerable. Seems to be like a huge sort of present."

Mike Newton, looking gaunt and changed, was running again as he pushed on toward the 500-mile mark. His black eyebrows stood out against his white face and, with his lips open as he breathed, his features had the stretched and distorted look of a mask. He had an electric, charged appearance as if he had taken himself out to some private edge. When the rest of us urged him on towards 500, he made a face—when you get that tired you don't take mileage for granted.

Joe Record began running with him over the last five miles. The two of them began to go faster and faster, streaking by everyone else on the track, as if Mike were a meteorite drawn by the ever-increasing gravitational force of the planet 500. They had run as hard as they could against each other for six days and nights and now, now that the outcome was irreversible, they ran side by side.

"Mike was in desperate condition," Joe said later. "I thought he might actually crack. That's why I ran through those last 19 laps with him. I began this game. I remembered when I was 19 and leaving home for the first time to hitchhike in Europe, then when I was 18, 17, 16, and the things I did at those ages. On lap twelve I asked how he was when he was twelve. Sometimes I'd talk because to have to answer takes too much. I also used my voice in certain kinds of ways so as not to be so hard to listen to.

"By the time we were ten, eight, seven, we got to be rather outrageous little brats, full of demands. Mike decided we ought to have champagne now. NOW! Five, four, three, two! We got to be completely bloody insane! 'If you're not going to give it to us we'll not run another bloody step!'"

On the last lap John Towers began sprinting along like crazy with the other two and then the three were flying over the track with the crowd cheering and then they were through, through at last.

"Ten miles to go was still a year away," Mike said a few days later. "Only when it was six laps away did I feel I could do it. I always felt I would not get there. On the very last lap I had no stomach. It was just gone, and in its place—free lift, amazing, no tiredness, as if shackles had been taken off, as if I were just starting off. It's not fair in running the way the leaders get all the highs and the runners behind are getting the stick.

"The instant I crossed the line it was like Christmas, birthday and New Year's and every conceivable good thing. When they landed on the moon—I know you can't compare this with *that*—but it's what I imagine they felt."

Who wasn't feeling good now that the end was at hand—even

the crippled ducks like myself beat their wings and took flight. I was ashamed to be running so fast and so freely at the end as if I had been malingering. I hadn't asked for it but all the same this wave of pure, rich, unfettered energy came and I ran as if I were just beginning. Looking over toward the stadium, I saw it was filled with a mass of people, dark green, blue and black in their wind breakers and parkas.

It was painful in a way to run the gauntlet past the grandstand. The applause and attention seemed too much; it broke in upon us too late. All that external stuff of the record breaking, the tears, the arms around each other as we formed twos and threes and fives and tramped round together—that was fine for us, but the world didn't really know about everything that came before. It was still a private event.

I don't know why it was all so amazing—amazing to feel so tired, so jaded, so bitter. What are you supposed to do when you are free again? I went away from everyone and lay down on my back and looked up at the sky. We were in heaven now and they had to confirm it by all manner of speeches and handshaking. The lord mayor was due at any moment in his fancy car, but this was better than anything, just lying there looking up at a sky as open and tranquil as it had been six days before.

Day Six

1.	Newton	505.04 miles
2.	Record	444.15
3.	Harney	432.47

4.	Morris	432.47
5.	Campbell	405.38
6.	Towers	377.79
7.	Choi	361.63
8.	Dixon	358.9
9.	Hayward	352.4
10.	Shapiro	346.72
11.	Parsons	343.24
12.	Collins	287.07
13.	Teesdale	284.58
14.	Holmes	276.38
15.	Emmons	269.67
16.	Richardson	256.0
17.	Blanton	234.13

LE GRIZZ

Don Kardong

L ike most stories, this one could begin almost anywhere. At conception. At birth. On the day I first began running. At the moment I discovered that, more than almost anything, I loved running through the woods, feeling an integral, primitive, part of the planet.

Perhaps the best point to begin, though, is at the moment I paid my $30 entry fee. Thirty dollars, after all, is not just three sawbucks. It signifies, rather, a commitment—in this case a commitment to run 50 miles. And so I hovered, a detached observer far above my checkbook, watching myself sign on the dotted line. Apparently I was actually going to do this thing.

For five years I had heard of Le Grizz, a 50-mile race in Montana. For love of this event, friends from Spokane, Washington, had driven long distances, camped in freezing weather, eluded ravenous bears and run, walked and ultimately dragged themselves to a distant finish line. Then, the trek completed, they had soaked in hot tubs and consumed beer and pizza until the pain subsided, leaving only the memories of an extraordinary adventure to relate to the folks back home. Most, it seemed, remained delirious for days, confessing to having enjoyed themselves. I always found this interesting. I had always been fascinated with ultramarathons (or "ultras"), had even considered running 70 miles from the English town where I lived to the ancient monument of Stonehenge. The point? Some sort of neo-Druid experience, I suppose, an athletic-religious-cosmic adventure. My friends thought I was nuts and talked me out of it.

Later I ran my first marathon, learning that it is not easy to run mile after mile after mile after mile. "If strange things can happen in a race of only 26 miles, what might lay in the void beyond fifty miles is a whole new world compared to the marathon," noted the Le Grizz entry form. "It is a world of new knowledge of oneself, of self-actualization and of brotherhood."

Obviously, someone penned this line in the delirium of post-race hot-tubbing. Still, the lure remained considerable. I can't explain why we choose to challenge the extremes of human endurance—climbing Mount Everest, swimming the English Channel or pursuing our own personal fantasy. But here's what I think: To explore boundaries is the reason for living.

For years, 50 miles sat on a back burner in my mind, simmering. Eventually, I succumbed.

The Night Before

There are moons and then, I swear, there are moons. On the evening before my first 50-miler, the moon that rose over the mountains behind the Spotted Bear Ranger Station was *real* moon.

Not a fat, lazy, mellow-yellow harvest moon or one of those fuzzy, sociable kind of orbs that smiles over urban landscapes. Rather, this was a piercing, ice-cold, nasty, I'm-the-eye-of-the-universe sort of moon that scattered the stars, scared wildlife, quieted the rocks and glared at our assembled group in the campground below. We were, this moon let us know, unlikely to get much sympathy from Mother Nature for what we were about to do.

The temperature was falling like a stone through ice water. Before dawn, it would hit 15 degrees F. October in the Rockies is a gamble with loaded dice.

"There is always the outside chance, this being Montana," noted the Le Grizz entry form, "of foul, horrible weather."

Actually, we were lucky. We didn't encounter any of the snow, sleet, wind or rain that visited the running of the Le Grizz in 1984. "Runners alternated between feelings of depression and stupidity as the start time approached," noted the report of that year's event.

This year it was simply cold. Naked cold. Dazzling-moon cold. You could see clearly a half-mile to the other side of the river. It was cold there, too.

Those who run ultras thrive on extremes. It is not enough, you see, to simply run 50 or 100 miles from point A to point B. We seek the added status that comes from tolerating extremes of temperature, navigating narrow trails and scoring thousands of feet of elevation change in regions where the air is impossibly thin.

To enter Le Grizz, I had been asked to sign the following: "I understand that participating in the Le Grizz 50-mile ultramarathon may subject me to injuries and illnesses, including but not limited to hypothermia, frostbite, heat stroke, heat exhaustion, physical exhaustion, animal attack, falling trees, road failure and vehicle accident."

Yes, I understand. And I paid my 30 bucks. I wasn't alone. Over 40 similarly disposed adults had signed up for Le Grizz, up from 25 the year before. Most gathered along with family and friends within a five-foot radius of the campfire at the Spotted Bear Campground, trying to carboload before the pasta froze.

The group included Rick Spady and Jim Pomroy, two Montana runners who between them had won all five previous Le Grizz runs. Spady, the faster of the two, held the Le Grizz record of 5:50:56. He also presided over the firewood, a job that seemed more a reflection of his nature than a specific obligation of the course-record holder.

I have stood around a fair number of campfires in my life, and they all seem blessed with the same purpose: to evoke memories, inspire philosophical ramblings and shake loose a few tall tales. Staring across the fire, one sees friends and strangers lost in thought. Their eyes reflecting the glow of sparks from the fire suggest the kindling of the mind. It is the look of human beings at peace, and also the look that flashes in the eyes of ax murderers just before the massacre. It is a look of ambiguous calm, and it appeared on the faces of the ultrarunners that evening.

As the night chill clamped down, most folks headed for the relative warmth of campers, tents and sleeping bags, leaving only a few seasoned ultrarunners around the fire to tell tales of Leadville, Western States and past Le Grizz struggles. They looked like woodsmen, hunters or perhaps creatures that came sneaking out of the woods in the middle of the night, eyes gleaming.

But they were simply runners of long races, about to begin another. Above them, the eye of the moon blasted its icy light across the wilderness, promising nothing but the indifference of Nature to human dreams.

The Start

We spent a rough night in the forest. In theory, I had the best accommodations within 50 miles of the starting line. The camper I had rented came complete with kitchen, toilet and sleeping areas for myself, my wife, Bridgid, and my two daughters, Kaitlin (age 4) and Catherine (age 2). More importantly, it had a heater. In spite of all this luxury, I thrashed around inside the thing all night, trying to find a spot where I could stretch out and sleep. Sleep deprivation became one more hardship to suffer in the spirit of ultrarunning.

Awakening on the morning of the run, I thought first of food. I ate cereal, cookies and whatever else seemed to speak the language of carbohydrates. Though not full, my stomach was engaged, hopefully giving my body a chance at surviving the hours and miles ahead.

Outside the camper, runners and friends scurried back and forth, puffing clouds of warm breath in the air while searching for food of their own. Many were dressed in custom-made yellow and black tights, the uniform of the day for those of us from Spokane. In the midst of my apprehension, the gaudy tights helped lighten the load. After pulling on a pair, I left the warmth of the camper and went hunting for the race director, Pat Caffrey. He was busy handing out race numbers at one end of the parking area. Caffrey—

the force behind Le Grizz—is the race director, the starter and the man in charge of almost everything. Most importantly, he writes the funny things about Le Grizz on the entry form and other race materials, helping the reader to forget what a gruesome thing a 50-mile run can be.

"Contrary to Yuppie Myth," wrote Caffrey about the atrocious weather that plagued Le Grizz runners in 1985, "people become wild animals, not environmentalists, when confronted with such a wilderness experience."

I understood that sentiment. After picking up my number and hustling to the line a few minutes before the eight o'clock starting time, as ready as I was going to be for this thing, I shivered relentlessly as Caffrey began a round of instructions, jokes and (at 15 degrees F!) information on how to buy leftover Le Grizz T-shirts.

"Brrrrr. Grrrrr," I muttered. Others around me agreed. "Today's temperature marks a Le Grizz record," Caffrey noted, grinning. Our frozen lips couldn't manage a comment. Finally, raising the starting weapon, a 12-gauge shotgun wound with electrician's tape, the man behind Le Grizz fired a single blast that echoed in the depths of the wilderness. Numb, we were off.

Zero to 10 Miles

The start of most road races is a flurry of arms, legs, elbows and adrenaline. The start of Le Grizz seemed more like the opening of Macy's doors on the day after Thanksgiving. People hurried, but within recognized bounds of propriety. We had time, plenty of time, to complete the task. It had been so complicated just getting going that morning—finding food, going to the bathroom, making sure cars would start (several needed considerable coaxing), deciding on the right combination of clothing, etc.—that I began to relate to Le Grizz as it should be. Not as a race, but as survival.

I *will* overcome all this. I will get to the finish. Other than finishing, I couldn't decide on an actual race goal. To win? To break six hours? I had nothing to base my expectations on, so I had settled on simply running the distance at a comfortable pace and scaling whatever obstacles lay in the road ahead.

After a mile or so, as the numbness in my quads, hands and face began to subside, I found myself running with Spady. We discussed ultramarathon training. Spady argued the value of the weekly long run instead of extremely high overall mileage. That system had kept him generally healthy and made him a top contender in races of 50 and 100 miles.

"People shouldn't worry so much about total mileage," said the course-record holder. "They'd do a lot better if they'd get out there and just keep going for six hours."

Long training runs, the kind that help ultrarunners, require a different perspective on the sport. Years ago I had tried adding 30-mile runs to my marathon training. One evening in 1977, I left home in the dark on an out-and-back course, 15 miles each way. After half an hour, I was running down a major highway, blinded by headlights and contemplating death. Thirty minutes later, I turned onto a country road, and things grew quiet. Only the breeze in the trees and my padding footsteps broke the silence. It was more like a dream than any training I was accustomed to. Suddenly an owl called "Whooooooo . . ." from a telephone pole.

I'm sorry, but this couldn't be called training. This was weirdness. It was also my last 30-mile training run for a decade. That's why I was so worried about Le Grizz. "Things get really *weird* after 35 miles," noted Von Klohe, a Spokane friend and ultrarunner who advised me on my Le Grizz training. Ultrarunners always say things like that. Then they chuckle.

As Spady and I ran along discussing ultramarathon training and racing, he reported the splits from his past Le Grizz runs. They made me nervous. The man was talking 6:10 and 6:20 mile pace—much faster than my own plans. Hearing these splits, I grew anxious for a reason to let him go. That opportunity came at about seven miles in the form of my support crew, my family. As we headed up a slight incline, I spotted them ahead.

The Le Grizz weekend represented a watershed for the Kardongs. It was our first night of camping together, at least if an evening in a heated home on wheels can be called camping. Things had gone well so far, but Bridgid and I both remained apprehensive about how well our two girls would tolerate six hours of riding in a camper while Dad slowly whittled himself to a nub. To get them in the spirit of things, I had put Kaitlin in charge of Dad's cookies.

Seeing my crew alongside the road at seven miles, I drifted off Spady's pace, slowed and stopped for aid. Kaitlin handed me a bag of unopened cookies. Bridgid was in the camper, changing Catherine's diaper.

A well-trained support crew is essential to success in ultramarathons. They provide quick access to fluids, food and emotional support. As I ripped open the package of cookies, wasting precious time and energy, I realized I had forgotten to give my crew any information about what it was they were supposed to do.

Up ahead, Spady was disappearing around a corner.

10 Miles—1:06:48

I'm not sure exactly how fast I expected to go through the various 10-mile checkpoints, but 1:06:48, including one aid stop and a pee break, seemed about right. I was running steadily, comfortably. Spady was nowhere in sight.

The main problem I had faced so far, other than an undertrained support crew, was clouds of dust from support-crew vehicles. It had been a dry summer and fall in the Rockies. As vehicles leapfrogged from aid station to aid station, they kicked up billowing clouds of dust, which threatened to smother those of us on foot.

Spady had speculated earlier that the dusty conditions would last until about 10 miles, when the bulk of the traffic would be behind us and the air would clear. He proved to be only slightly off the mark. After 10 miles, dust and traffic began to fade, replaced by the full beauty of the countryside through which Le Grizz travels.

Hungry Horse Reservoir sits on the western side of the continental divide in northwestern Montana, just south of Glacier Park. Waters from here flow in convoluted fashion through Montana, Idaho, Canada and Washington, eventually joining the Columbia River. The Le Grizz course follows a road along the southwest side of Hungry Horse Reservoir, affording participants still in control of their faculties an exquisite view across to the Great Bear Wilderness area.

The sight itself is worth the drive (though perhaps not a 50-mile run) , especially in the fall. In this part of the country, most of the conifers just hunch their shoulders and settle in for the winter with no major transformation. The tamaracks, though, change from green to gold, then drop their needles like any deciduous tree. At the same time, aspens, birches, cottonwoods and alders are busy turning color among the evergreens, splashing their hues across the hills. the aspens, in particular, stand out among the forest giants, brilliant gold, shimmering with the slightest breeze as if charged with electricity.

On this day, too, the moon had joined the scenery, preceding us most of the way. Hanging just above the trees, it had grown less and less harsh, deferring to the ascending sun and the blue sky. The moon had, I imagined, given up glaring at us, stumbled and simply accepted the lunacy of human beings.

Now that the dust had settled, running through this scenery became distinctly pleasurable. Fifty miles began to seem possible, reasonable, even easy. The view was gorgeous, my legs felt strong and the temperature had warmed to a comfortable level. I was really enjoying myself.

The attraction of Le Grizz—the combination of scenery and challenge—grew clearer. It was the ability to run without effort through natural splendor. It was the calm of the forest and the joy of self-propulsion. It was the combination of two loves, running and wilderness, that induced euphoria. I smiled. This was wonderful. And then I hit the first big uphill. I wouldn't call it a monster— just a steady, continuous upgrade of perhaps a half-mile. When it had passed, my euphoria had dimmed. I was no longer convinced of my ability to travel another 40 miles. My quads had complained on the way up, the first signal of problems lying ahead.

With five hours of running left, the joy of the forest began to give way to the reality of the long road through it. Misery would come later. For now, miles 10 to 20 became a task, a goal within a goal: I must *get* to the 20-mile mark. Mentally, the secret to running 50 miles lies with the process of putting miles behind you. Ten miles represents one chunk, 20 miles another. It's a little like filling a garbage bag with aluminum cans. Crush the can, throw it in the bag. Crush another, throw it in the bag. Crush it, bag it, crush it, bag it, crush it, bag it. This is not an elegant process, and at times it seems both endless and meaningless. Eventually, though, the bag is full.

At 13 miles, my support crew appeared again, better prepared this time. I took a swig of defizzed Pepsi, asked them to meet me in another three miles or so and trotted off. They showed up again at 17 miles, where Kaitlin handed me a half glass of Pepsi and Bridgid announced that I was ahead of Spady. "I don't think so," I answered. "He went ahead at the first stop, and I haven't passed him."

"The only guy I've seen is that other runner," she said, referring to someone who was running as part of a relay team. "I'm sure you're ahead of everyone else." "I don't think so."

I downed the pop and headed off again. Whether I led or not seemed irrelevant. I needed to relax, conserve energy, try to go with the flow. I hadn't even reached halfway yet, but already the tightness was growing, from my stomach to my knees.

20 Miles—2:12:58

Twenty miles. A long Sunday morning training run, the kind that drains my legs for at least a couple of days. This time, though,

20 miles marked only the beginning. Thirty more lay ahead. The split time was encouraging. My pace had held up nicely for the second 10, but was I making a big mistake? Just prior to 20 miles, I had passed the relay runner. Now I began to suspect that Bridgid was right: I was in first place. I couldn't figure out what had happened to Spady; I began to suspect that he and his crew had played some kind of trick. Perhaps they were leaving me to my own devices, the neophyte ultrarunner, to dig my own grave. Was I running too fast?

Whatever the answers, I consciously slowed myself down and concentrated on getting to 30 miles. Seeing my support crew a short while later, I stopped for more fluid and a molasses cookie, hoping to delay the complete depletion of my dwindling energy reserves.

Every marathoner knows that at a point near 20 miles, the body sends out notices saying, "Enough already." Running becomes geometrically more difficult, fatigue seems to encompass the body, collapse is imminent and depression sets in. All this happens between one toe-off and the next heel-strike, don't ask me how. Marathoners call it "hitting the Wall."

In an effort to avoid the Wall, ultramarathoners eat on the run. I hoped that the occasional sugary pop and cookie that I consumed would do the trick. However, any attempt to keep the body adequately supplied with energy during a 50-miler can meet with only partial success, and I knew I would soon be running on empty. As early as 20 miles, I had begun to feel slightly dizzy, moderately disoriented.

An ultramarathon teaches you, as the Zen masters have always insisted, that body and mind are inseparable. The mind does not sit in the skull, happily piloting the body from checkpoint to checkpoint, detached from the organism's needs. As the body staggers, so does the mind. They are, my friends, connected. If you don't believe me, try a 50-miler.

Earlier my smoothly running body had made me feel euphoric. Now it was doing a bang-up job of foisting paranoia on the mind. Hungry grizzlies, I grew convinced, were watching me run. The Le Grizz entry form (a.k.a. Pat Caffrey) says the following about midrace wildlife: "The road is lightly traveled in October and goes through wild, mountainous country where grizzly bears still roam. Other mammals, such as deer, elk, moose, black bear, mountain lion, bobcat and coyote, are common." In this year's final instructions, Caffrey had added the following: "The Montana Department of Fish, Wildlife and Parks has been trapping our grizzly bears from the west side of the reservoir. Six have been removed recently. If this continues, you may be running 'Le Traps!'"

Ultrarunners may be able to laugh at adversity, but when you get right down to it, grizzly bears are not funny. Like sharks, they eat people, and generally without benefit of music.

"Don't worry," a ranger at Glacier Park, Montana, once told me. "Grizzlies will only attack if you surprise them, invade their territory or come between them and their cubs." Three things, I explained to him, that a runner could do without realizing it.

A grizzly bear can run up to 30 miles an hour, meaning it could give Ben Johnson a head start and still feast on his carcass at 80 meters. Grizzlies are both unpredictable and quick on their feet.

So there I was, running out in front of the ultraparade, a

mostly solitary figure traveling through the wilderness and enjoying the scenery, when it suddenly dawned on me that I heard crackling noises in the bushes.

I've spent enough time in the woods to know that even a tiny animal, a chipmunk, for example, can make a lot of noises. A bear, then ought to sound like a rock slide as it snaps branches, crushes dry leaves and generally bullies its way through the forest. So argued my rational mind, insisting on its ability to make an objective judgment about the crackling of twigs. But, I tell you again, the mind is connected to the body—in this case a body with a fuel tank approaching zero.

The grizzly could be standing very still, waiting to run me down, the mind mused. He's probably watching me right now. My black-spotted tights, which accent the giraffeness of my legs, are probably invoking some sort of predatory response in the bear *at this very moment.*"

In a past Le Grizz, one of the Spokane runners had spotted a pile of fresh bear dung in the road. ("Right about this point in the race," my weakening mind noted.) Another Spokane runner had responded to the crackling and crashing in the underbrush by stopping to throw rocks, a sure sign of glycogen depletion. I told myself that, should I suddenly encounter a big Yogi I would respond more appropriately, which meant . . . well, anyway, I would not throw rocks. Meanwhile, as I continued toward the halfway mark, I tried to relax and imagine that the sounds I was hearing were made by chipmunks, birds and other creatures that used to delight Snow White and not by the sort of animal that can remove a runner's head with a single swipe of its paw.

LE GRIZZ / DON KARDONG

Marathon—2:56:14

In the 1976 Olympics, I ran the marathon in 2:11:16. Thus, a time 45 minutes slower than that should not have pleased me, but it did. Passing the marathon mark in 2:56:14 went much more smoothly than I might have expected.

There is no such thing as an "easy" marathon. Twenty-six miles of easy running still produce sore, tight, fatigued muscles and a mind that is tired, scattered and testy. Body and mind have had it. This, the duo agree, would be a good time to stop. In the very first Le Grizz Ultramarathon in 1982, runners crossed this point, indicated by "26.2 miles" written in red paint on the road immediately observed an arrow pointing down the road with the inscription: THE UNKNOWN. I imagine Pat Caffrey on the evening before the run, grinning devilishly as he wrote this. Passing the marathon point this time, I had several thoughts. One, I was *more* than halfway. I had fewer miles to go now than I had already covered. The feeling was similar to what I've experienced during a track workout after completing six out of 10 440-yard repeats. An odd sort of relief blossomed. The garbage bag was more than half full. Two, I needed to *get* there. In an ultra, the satisfaction of reaching a mile point is short-lived. I wanted to reach the next major milestone immediately.

Three, I needed a potty stop. My stomach had been bothering me for the past 10 miles, and I thought a trip to the bathroom would help. Seeing my support crew ahead, I pulled over and headed into the van for relief.

There's a Disney cartoon in which Goofy puts on a pair of

stretch pants without taking off his snow skis. That's how I felt trying to do my business in the tiny camper toilet. I figured afterwards it must have taken at least three minutes, most of which involved logistics rather than function. I spent thirty seconds or so convincing Kaitlin and Catherine that they didn't need to visit me during this activity.

Back on the road I felt much better. Part of me worried that Spady might have caught and passed me during my prolonged pit stop, but mostly I was concerned about monitoring vital signs rather than staying ahead of anyone.

30 Miles—3:25:20

I didn't take much solace from reaching the 30-mile checkpoint. I could only think: 20 miles left—the length of my Sunday morning long run. Too many miles.

Even the time, 3:25, evoked no particular response. More importantly, I had forgotten to share some important information with Bridgid. I had meant to warn her about the drastic personality deterioration I expected would soon strike me. When blood sugar drops, the "personality," a supposedly fixed set of human traits and attributes, proves to be about as permanent as Mount St. Helens. Ordinarily reasonable, pleasant folks become nasty, whining, hopeless idiots.

This once happened to a friend of mine who, preparing for a marathon, decided to follow the carbohydrate-depletion routine while living in the vicinity of his wife, which proved a big mistake. When she served a meal that didn't meet his standards, he complained loudly and stomped off to the nearest supermarket. An

LE GRIZZ / DON KARDONG

hour later he returned, looking sheepish. "I went to the store, but I didn't eat anything," he confessed. "I just walked around."

"For 45 minutes?" his wife asked incredulously. It was true. This is fairly typical behavior for a runner whose leg muscles have cannibalized all the body's fuel. It's best to steer clear of such folks.

My support crew, though, had agreed to stay with me. Even if I became so rude and disagreeable that they would rather hand me over to the grizzlies. We were clearly entering a danger zone of intrafamily relationships. When the camper appeared again, I vowed to issue a warning. "Do you need anything?" Bridgid asked sweetly.

"No, but I'm going to start getting nasty pretty soon," I answered obliquely. Bridgid has watched me slowly deplete before. She knew exactly what I meant.

For the next few miles, the road seemed to climb steadily, rising fairly high above the reservoir. The going got tough, and I labored hard at it. At 33 miles I stopped for fluids, nearly threw up from the ensuing nausea and began walking to regain my equilibrium. Just then Bridgid pulled up beside me in the camper. "I think you slowed down a bit," she said innocently, forgetting about my increasing depletion. I stared ahead morosely and kept walking. Fortunately, I wasn't carrying a weapon. Suddenly, some kind of large bird, a pheasant perhaps, took flight from the bushes. It may have been frightened, but I was terrified. My heartbeat soared.

I began to feel the way l had at the Ultimate Runner, a pentathlon of running events I had entered a year earlier, when I reached the final miles of the marathon. I would travel one mile at a time, reward myself with a short walking break and a drink at each mile marker. I thought, a similar system might help me get through Le Grizz, so I asked my support crew to meet me at every mile marker.

40 Miles—4:38:17

I am entering a world not of sight or sound, but of mind. And the signpost up ahead says: LE GRIZZ—40 MILES. "Ultramarathons are for the patient and calculating runner," says the Le Grizz entry form. "You are in charge of your body, your mind, your run." Well, maybe. At 40 miles, though, it sure as hell didn't feel like it.

The next five miles would prove the hardest of the day. Along with the general beating my legs had taken, my stomach continued to rebel and my mind drifted like an explorer without a compass. At one moment I'd feel certain that I could win my first 50-miler in less than six hours. The next moment I would be struggling against the urge to walk the rest of the way. For some bizarre reason, a good part of my concern during these miles focused on having Bridgid stop the camper *exactly* at each mile mark, not 50 or 100 meters down the road. For Bridgid, though, driving along searching for the white mile marks in the road proved to be incompatible with supervising two camperbound preschoolers. Mile after mile, she missed them. And mile after mile I repeated my whining request that she drive to the exact mile-marker locations.

"I don't know why it's so important to me," I told her at 43 miles, "but please stop right on the next mark."

Later on, a Snickers bar in one hand and a beer in the other, this kind of behavior seems so foolish. Unfortunately, after 40-plus miles of an ultramarathon, it seems divinely ordained. It was crucial that Bridgid stop where I directed. Closing in on the 44-mile mark, I grew incensed. Bridgid was not there! After all my begging, she still wasn't on the mark! I cursed. I may have even picked up the pace a bit, anticipating that I'd see the camper around the next turn. She wasn't there either. One more turn. Still not there. Suddenly I realized the awful truth: Bridgid had missed stopping at 44 miles altogether. I would have to run all the way to 45 miles!

God, what a cruel, cruel world, in which a man has to run *two miles* without a support crew. I screamed something into the forest. Something about Bridgid. To this day, only the trees and wildlife know what I howled.

I wanted to cry, to stop, to lie down and never get up again. Somehow, though, I kept going, step after painful step. Finally, an eon or so later, I reached 45 miles. "I can't believe you missed the last mile-point," I whimpered.

"I'm sorry," Bridgid replied. She seemed sincere.

My time at 45 miles was 5:18:40. I drank another half-glass of defizzed Pepsi and walked down the road. Ten seconds later, I threw up.

"It never always gets worse," Dan Brannen, a long-time ultra-running aficionado, had explained to me prior to Le Grizz. He suggested I should remember those words when the downward spiral of bad to even-worse-than-that seemed unbroken, infinite. "Eventually," said Brannen, "something will get better."

And it was that advice, that odd nugget of wisdom, that rang truer than anything else at 45 miles. It never always gets worse. We're talking about me now, not just ultramarathons. Or at least me in the downward spiral. "Survive," we tell ourselves and others in the throes of despair. "Endure. It will get better."

Perhaps the attraction of ultrarunning lies in the simple distillation of this: the ability to envision a distant goal—another time and place when things will be better—and to survive the worst until then. This vision embraces both the survival instinct that unites us to other creatures and the imagination and willpower that catapults us above them. "I *will* make it," says the determined mind, and the body grows convinced.

Suddenly, as if on cue, I felt better. I rallied. Only five miles to go.

I sensed again that I might win this thing, might even break six hours. Those particular aspirations had been buried beneath a stack of miles for the last three hours. Even now, the truly relevant goal was to keep going at any pace without walking. The final miles were more or less a blur of hills, sore quads, elevated spirits, low blood sugar and human conviction. The last two seemed especially tough, as I skipped the final aid station in the hope of breaking six hours.

"Dad looks pretty good again, doesn't he?" Bridgid said to Catherine, who was now riding happily in the front seat with Kaitlin.

"Yeah," she answered cheerfully in two-year-old-ese, "he no throw up now."

"In a 50-miler," says the Le Grizz entry form, "one competes against one's own limits, not someone else's limits. To finish is to win."

After five hours, 58 minutes and 37 seconds of running, walking, pit stops, vomiting, despair and determination, it was over. I had won. I finished.

Epilogue

Exactly two steps after crossing the Le Grizz finish line, I stopped. Bridgid escorted me to the camper, where I found I couldn't climb high enough to get inside. My quads simply, absolutely refused to lift me. Eventually Bridgid managed to push me inside, where I pulled on warm-ups and commenced to eating. Soon Spady dropped by, looking much, much better than I felt. He had struggled with stomach problems all day, but still finished second in 6:19:57.

In chatting with other finishers, I discovered that one had actually seen a grizzly at the 18-mile mark. So was it depletion-induced paranoia or a sixth sense that told me something was drooling in the bushes as my tights flashed by? All the runners who completed Le Grizz were eager to share their adventures, but I noticed they were even more eager to begin eating unhealthy things—candy, pop, ho-ho's, fried chicken. Someone who has just run 50 miles is in no mood for alfalfa sprouts. We had paid our dues, expended tens of thousands of calories. It was time to chow down.

After we had consumed beer, chicken and assorted junk food and watched a moose graze across a lake near the finish area, the sun was dipping toward the horizon. Caffrey finally called us to huddle together for the awards ceremony.

In an event as personally challenging as a 50-miler, organizers seem to feel that, since they told you "to finish is to win," the least they can do is prove they mean it. Everyone gets a trophy.

I accepted my award with pride—it's the only trophy I've chosen to display in public. It has a shellacked wooden base and a figure of a grizzly bear standing on its hind legs, looking fearsome. That bear has, I imagine, just spotted a skinny human being in yellow-and-black-tights running through its domain. For a week after Le Grizz, I hobbled down the hallways of the building in downtown Spokane where I work, hoping someone would question the reason behind my limp. ("Oh, that? Nothing serious, really. Just tired legs from a 50-mile run. That's right, 50.") Gradually, my muscles began to rebuild. In a strange way, though, I relished the residual pain—evidence of my journey through the world beyond the marathon.

And after that?

The Le Grizz entry form says this about the post-race period. "You might feel burned out for four days as a result of energy depletion. Then comes some euphoria." Spady had put it differently when we chatted right after the run.

"I've got some real bad news for you," he said, grinning somewhere beneath his Fu Manchu. "In about three days you're going to think you had fun out there today."

He was wrong. It took almost a week.

TO THE LIMIT AND BEYOND

Kenny Moore

"The struggle itself toward the heights is enough to fill a man's heart. One must imagine Sisyphus happy."—Albert Camus

For exactly 21 minutes, it was nostalgic. We padded past the same cane fields and pastures of red cows and snowy egrets that we'd known three years before. This was the second Great Hawaiian Footrace, commencing in April of 1981 on Oahu's north shore. It would take the 46 entrants of assorted ability, sex and motive a lap and a half around the island, then (and this was new) conclude with a lap of Maui, 18 days of running in all, a total of 500,000 meters or 313 miles.

Every day we would camp in beach parks, except for the four

nights we hit Honolulu, when we would be lodged at the venerable Moana Hotel. Every morning we would load our tent city into vans and run from 10 to 23 miles to the next chosen stand of ironwoods or palms, the next sapphire bay.

But rumination on these blessings or even my smug recollection of actually having won the race in 1979, ended for good after three miles. John McCormack, 32, a fireman from Brooklyn, took the pace from seven minutes per mile, which had been our average throughout the first race, to 6:30, and a couple of miles later to 6:00, and then 5:50. I ran a step behind him, the others falling away, and surreptitiously checked the times between mileposts. It was a long race. So even though the day was cool at 70 degree and the wind was at our backs, the pace seemed an extravagant risk. The eighth mile was a 5:43. I eased and McCormack went smoothly on to win the 18-mile first leg in 1:55:38. I was a minute back, feeling mildly betrayed. McCormack had run 15 minutes faster than my old friend Leon Henderson and I had over the same first leg in 1979. In fact, Henderson and I had controlled much of the pace in the inaugural adventure. As a result, those weeks, in memory at least, were colored less by competition than by discovery. We had marveled at Hawaii's varied landscape and at vivid characters among the participants, not least of which was the race's originator, Dr. Jack Scaff. Competition is alien to Scaff. His joy is not to vanquish but to teach, to astonish, even if he had to make something up to do it. Scaff was running with us, talking a great race. The real organizer of the trek was his wife, Donna, who during the running parts of our days directed a loyal crew in handing out drinks and ice from our accompanying van every three and a half miles.

I'd felt a childish relief at returning the rental car I'd had for a week of acclimation. I didn't even have to drive any more now, only run and be given catered dinners, entertainment and free electrocardiograms. Well, not quite free. The entry fee of $1,200 covered the food and lodging. The electrocardiograms were for those of us who were subjects in a research study on the effect of our mileage on heart enzymes. On four mornings we surrendered 25 CC of blood to Rudy Dressendorfer, Ph.D. of the William Beaumont Hospital near Detroit. As well, there were less painful nutrition and urine studies.

But the main worry now was McCormack. "I'm going to win it," he had said in a letter to Donna Scaff. "I was third in the first one, and that race showed me my potential for this day-after-day running. I've trained hard, and I'm going to take it to him."

On the first day McCormack had slowed slightly as it grew warmer, but he seemed to recover well, putting on a blue rain suit after finishing and staying out of the sun. My thoughts were more of myself. I had found that when McCormack was out in front and racing, no matter if it was the first day, I was incapable of not trying to stay close. This was nostalgia of a sort, too. I had run in the 1968 and 1972 Olympic marathons. In recent years, because of lingering injuries and the press of travel, I had raced little, beginning to imagine it a phase I had departed. Now I was sound and in fair condition. And, it seemed, the battle reflexes were still there.

Yet fitness and competitiveness wouldn't be enough. Unlike almost any other event since the transcontinental Bunion Derby of the 1920s, the Great Hawaiian Footrace calls for hard running every day (an average of 17.5 miles). Thus its structure (to the chagrin of Jack Scaff, who hadn't imagined that what he'd conceived as a three-week running vacation would turn out this way) resembles bicycle races such as the Tour de France. But running is absolutely not like cycling in one crucial respect. Runners pound the roads. Cyclists do not. The shock fatigue that accumulates from absorbing about two and a half times one's own weight with every footfall prevent runners from being able to do the five-to eight-hour daily grinds of cycling tours. It is also why runners can train only about 40 percent as long as swimmers, rowers or other athletes who don't constantly slam parts of themselves against the ground.

Many runners, including this one, need one or two or three days of easy jogging after every hard or long run to recover fully from the pounding. The Great Hawaiian Footrace, because it allows no such days, presents a clear problem of managing one's own disintegration. "Our results from the 1979 race," said Dressendorfer, who has found the event an unsurpassed opportunity to study the biochemistry of fatigue," show that once someone's legs are sore, they stay sore the rest of the way. There is no recovery from any breakdown." Even the two-day rest we would get after 10 days of racing, before we flew to Maui, wouldn't be enough to restore road-pounding muscle.

Every day was a race, but a race that couldn't be run so hard that it jeopardized future days.

We were at Mokulela Beach Park. I swam above a beautiful reef, but I grew cold almost at once, the sea less hospitable than before. Jack Scaff's son, Jackson, 13, was stung by a Portuguese man-of-war and sat in camp fighting the pain: There were broad welts across his back as if he'd been whipped.

In cool mists we began the second day, sleepy, stiff, chuckling about Scaff's lecture the night before on how to deal with attacking dogs, a bane to runners everywhere. "They won't bite anything that submits to their territoriality, and the sign of submission is getting lower than their heads," he said in perfect seriousness. "So stop if they chase you, and crouch down . . ."

By then he was shouting through a storm of heckling. "You mean I gotta choose between being bitten in the leg and being bitten in the face?" said Henderson.

"And what about cats?" yelled McCormack.

After three miles the road became the rutted, twisting track across Kaena Point. The deeper holes were filled with water. Black lava rocks rise out of the sea, and the scene is one of compelling severity, but I didn't catch more than a glimpse or two of it during those six miles because I was desperately concentrating on the footing. Five of us alternated the lead. Then I began to make mistakes, choosing the wrong side of a hole to skirt and getting hung up in the brush, sliding into mud up to my ankles. Once I went down, a rock chewing up my palm. I staggered onto the smooth road for the last nine miles in forth place. Kris Krichko of Eugene, OR, a fine cross-country skier, ran powerfully ahead. I decided to just roll gently in. Save it for tomorrow, a 23-mile day. I took shelter from the wind behind Don Zaph of Boise, Idaho. Then McCormack weakened up ahead and we caught him. I didn't pick up the pace but found myself alone in second at the finish in Walanae, where I washed off about two pounds of dried mud in the ocean.

We were divided into serious competitors, who would eventually be ranked on a basis of accumulated time, and "adventurers" who timed themselves and could stop their watches while they ate, swam or shopped. Sometimes three hours went by between the hard racers and these happy explorers who arrived with word of bittersweet-nugget milk shakes. While the field came in I lay on the shell-strewn beach and thought carefully about this McCormack. I had gotten my minute back, so we were even on elapsed time. If this were to develop into a sustained duel, I had to come to some conclusions that would let me take advantage of my strengths and minimize his. Again, the heat at the end of the run seemed to reach him. His best marathon was 20 minutes slower than mine, but that was offset by his durability. In 1979 he had won most of the last legs, finishing freshest of all. Though I could probably run faster on a given leg, I would pay for such speed with successive days of vulnerability to injury. The strategy suggested by all this was to stay close, if possible, and wait, and perhaps on a hot day to take back with one strong bite what he had nibbled away.

The dawn of the third day was clear and still and dry. "I guarantee you heat," said Scaff. We were off by 6:30, down the busy Farrington Highway. After an hour, the lead pack of five marched through 10 miles of cane fields, huge trucks roaring past our elbows. A wind came up against us and we all drafted along behind McCormack. Instead of sun, there was a cool, refreshing rain.

I should have been running second. But it was comfortable back in fifth in the lee of muscular Rudi Schmidt of LaVerne, Calif. I looked up with seven miles to go and saw the others had let McCormack get away. Where were their instincts? As we turned toward Pearl City, putting the wind at our side, I tried to catch him. I couldn't. He won by a minute, kept strong by the chill.

I sat among the 46 blue duffel bags in the beach-park shelter and rested, taking note of the pattern of our days. Already it seemed fixed, natural. There was the early hard run into not quite irreparable fatigue, then some recovery (which took longer each day), and then this planning, this observation of my fellows in the hope of discerning—what? A lesson? Or simply other patterns? I ran and then reflected. It was a rhythm that embraced the primary human capacities of action and thought, the body/mind split that has always seemed so fundamental to scholar-athletes and philosophers. This cycle was embedded in the mythic punishment of Sisyphus, the endless sequence of pushing his rock up the hill, watching it topple and crash away into the abyss, and walking down in its wake, pondering his fate.

We had only 14 miles to do the next day, from Pearl Harbor through Honolulu to Waikiki, so we waited until eight to start, to let the morning rush hour die down. Didn't work. McCormack took off after four miles. I used him as wind-break, but to keep him I had to run hard. He ran on the right, on the edge of traffic. I hate that. My mind's eye kept seeing a cement truck, its driver blinded by the sun, collecting us on the grille. Whenever a rumbling horn sounded behind us, I'd hop into the ditch where the shoulder should have been. McCormack strode on unconcerned, apparently used to such things on Brooklyn streets. Twice trucks missed him by no more than six inches. Each time he turned and gave me an offended look, as if it were their fault.

It was hot. With three miles to go, he ran into Ala Moana Park for a drink. I kept going. I figured he'd catch up. He didn't, and I won my first leg of the race. He was only a few seconds back, but because of his pace the next guys were seven minutes behind. It was a two-man race.

On the beach I tried to make sense of McCormack's strength. His absence of fear seemed an example of how intense effort can cloud awareness of outside forces, even slaughter by truck. So was he therefore closer to his limit than I? I had no real faith in my reading of him. We were different people, the Eastern, gregarious, beer-drinking fireman so solemn in his run, and the withdrawn Westerner who seemed to fill with confidence only when on the road.

He was a good man, and I couldn't imagine our competition becoming so bitter that it would interfere with my affection for him. Yet we seldom talked. I liked a little sun; he kept to the shade. We had different confidants among the field. We must, to each other, have seemed the archetypal competitors, the guys you always seem to have to face, very possibly better than you, a challenge to the ability to dig deep and the ability not to panic.

The next day was 17 miles east from Waikiki, over two tough hills, the finish at Makapuu Beach Park. The early pace was easy, McCormack liking to warm to his task, but after six miles he was in the lead and pushing. The head wind was strong, so I got on his back and let him do all the work. I felt small pangs of conscience at this occasionally, but it was a race, and he didn't seem to mind, never trying to shake me off with surges. We wouldn't have gone nearly as fast if I had led. My thighs were not sore, but pre-sore, so I told myself that if we went really fast, I'd let him go.

McCormack carries his arms rather high and they swing across his chest in a relaxed pendulum action, balancing the long sweep of his legs. Even protected behind him I was often rocked back by the 20-knot trade wind, but he shoved through it without panic. His legs are thickly muscled for a runner, so he has a low center of gravity and terrific balance. He can run within an inch of a curb or guard rail for a mile and not touch it. In all of these things I am his opposite.

For two days we had run like this. For weeks afterward the details of his shirtless back would appear in my dreams. He has a birthmark, a small area of skin that doesn't tan, on his spine six inches above his waist, exactly in the shape of Great Britain. Liverpool is there, and the mouth of the Thames, and a freckle for London. "My mother always told me that was a Christmas tree," he would say later. So smooth was his high-kicking stride that this spot never moved. It just shifted and stretched a little over his relentlessly operating back muscles.

After 10 miles he eased slightly, and I knew I could hold him for this day. The finish was downhill. I let him sprint away to a three-second win in 1:42:47, thinking that his work into the wind had earned him a moral five minutes.

I was sore that night. The race seemed more than ever a test of predictive, extrapolative powers. What would the effect be, weeks and hundreds of miles, later, of decisions of pace and effort, following or leading?

Scaff has seemed to ignore the race up front. Now, learning we were 56 minutes faster over the first 89 miles than we'd been in 1979, he narrowed his eyes at us as if we were possessed, and he was not sure it was healthy. He sat on ironwood roots with me, watching the first sun. "Why do you do this race?" he asked. He seemed almost upset. "And why so hard?"

I couldn't explain. When I spoke of the land, the people, the escape, it all seemed to come to mush.

"Do you ever think, 'God, racing through back roads in Hawaii, what a comedown for an Olympic marathoner?'"

"No," I said. "It isn't a comedown. The imperatives are the same in any race. I get in a situation like this one with John, and I don't think of anything but what is necessary to have a chance to win. Then afterward I'm as amazed as you at what we're doing. Especially the destructiveness of the race." He didn't seem much comforted.

Extrapolation kept right on going for me that evening, expanding to include foreshadowing of later years, of age. I had a career's experience of gauging levels of tiredness to summon for decisions in this race. But what would I call on to know whether it was better to kick and bite against the onset of decline or to accept it?

As an Olympian, had I ever regarded my running as affirmation of vigor and youth, a denying of death? No. It had been a chase. The thrill was in improvement, in a discipline that was difficult. If there was defiance then, it was that I ran to set myself at a distance from the compromising mass. That aloofness was characteristic, but I was too full of life to think that I was opposing death. Death was myth.

Day six was 21 miles over the steepest hills we would run on Oahu. McCormack started slowly. I lead by 200 yards at four miles, impressed at the good a night's sleep could do. But within a mile he came past, Krichko with him, at what seemed five-minute pace. I couldn't stay with them. The hills were making my legs worse. They beat me by six minutes through a cool rain. I finished in a sour, desolate mood. McCormack had the lead on elapsed time and he seemed to be growing stronger every day. I knew I was not. I had to forcibly remind myself that there were 12 running days left: One could not make partial-surrender statements so early, even to oneself.

Later, walking the Kualoa Park, once a region sacred to Hawaiians, a city of refuge for the hunted of the island's other districts, I found myself considering the athlete's way of keeping hopeful, of ignoring the odds. In competition you suspend disbelief. You go hard all the way when opponents seem out of range, just on the chance you'll do well.

Yet that is in contrast with dispassionate, logical behavior.

Yogi Berra's "it's never over until it's over" is sheer tautology to an academic intellect. It is sacred tenet to the athlete.

Weeks later, on the radio, I would hear Goose Gossage railing profanely against sportswriters, and the worst printable thing he could think to call them was "negative." He couldn't stomach their not understanding that players had to be irrationally positive. It's the only rational way to play. He seemed right. Writers seldom understand. But neither did he acknowledge that their writing and his play are on opposite sides of that chasm referred to earlier: thought vs. action, scientific vs. partisan. It seemed in that light that he was upset at nature, furious with the only universe we know.

I loved to run with the wind. We had only 14 miles to cover on the seventh day, and I was stiff and uncoordinated, but at the four-mile water station I was done gulping first, so I led. It was a level run, with the wind pressing on our right shoulders and the sea always near. It crossed my mind that as McCormack had gone hard yesterday, it wouldn't be entirely dumb to keep some pressure on him today. He slipped back with five miles left, and my aching left thigh and calf seemed to hold steady at 5:45 pace; so I got back 45 seconds, stopping at the end of the leg beside a field of apprehensive cows.

I was groggy the next morning heading into a 20-miler, but McCormack wasn't. I wanted it hot. It began to rain. I had to let him go after nine miles. But he only ran out to a 200-yard lead, then hung there. The sun came out. I caught him through Haleiwa, with two and a half miles to go. We were like boxers, punched out in the late rounds. I couldn't get away from him. He couldn't get away from me. We finished together in 2:01.

After we crossed the line, we sank down, hands on knees. We chose the same moment to look up at each other. His eyes were so unguarded it seemed I could see his soul. And surely he mine. "I promised myself I couldn't have any beer if I didn't at least keep up with you at the end," he said.

"God, you're getting serious," I said.

The next day was our second passage around rugged Kaena Point. I felt so heavy-legged and weary that the object became not to break an ankle. He had 100 yards when we regained the pavement. I caught him quickly. I sensed his weakness and tried to muscle away in the four miles remaining. I had a cramp in my back from waving my arms to keep my balance among the rocks, but I tried as hard as I could. He refused to crack. I won, but only by 24 seconds. He still lead by two and a half minutes overall.

The first thing he said afterward was, "That 22 miles tomorrow is going to be a son of a bitch." I took that to mean that he intended to make it so. It would be our last run on Oahu. I told myself I would take anything he had to give, because then I had two days to at least partially heal. I needed them. My right thigh burned at the touch, even of ice. My left hip seemed to have some sand or broken glass in it. Oddly, I had no blisters.

Knowing what was to come, and having made some peace with it, McCormack and I had lunch together. He revealed his strategy: "When Kenny's down, you got to kick him in the side."

I warmed up for 10 minutes the next morning. They day seemed to promise heat, though Scaff said it would be wet. I had decided that if McCormack wished to start with a couple of seven-minute miles, I would start with sixes and make him choose between his normal pattern and giving me a two-minute lead.

I got a pretty good rhythm going, that sense of everything meshing, and somehow ignored the traffic on the hateful Farrington Highway. At the three-and-a-half-mile aid station, McCormack was within 50 yards. At seven he was still there. I got a good handful of ice under my hat and kept on. Cane smoke hung in the air, and the sun began to tell. I was on 5:40 pace by now and running emotionally. I was using my special, prideful past. I was an Oregon runner. I knew what it was to cast off all fears and blaze the last part of a race or workout as if it were the last you'd ever run.

I looked back at 11 miles and couldn't see him. I had near spasms in my back. But this was the chance I'd looked for, to really get some time ahead. I worked the hills and rolling road through the cane, fought the traffic into Ewa Beach and had the energy to sprint the last 200 yards.

I was weighed and had lost eight pounds, going from 151 to 143 in the two hours and 13 minutes, not an exceptional volume. But I didn't recover very quickly. I felt pretty rocky, and I kept feeling it. Dressendorfer, a medical physiologist, had me drink Coke, water and beer, and pointed toward a canebrake to give him a urine specimen.

I have a vivid memory of pushing into the scratchy cane. The stalks were an inch thick and purple, and the russet earth was muddy, and the urine filling the plastic cup was heart-blood red.

I walked back to Dressendorfer, a little shaken, for in my 38 years this had never happened before. I gave him the cup. "We'll follow up on this," he said eagerly, the scientist aroused. I had more beers, four to be exact, and got into a pain-liberated mood, proud, in the perverse way of distance runners, of how I'd used everything. Measured by its toll, I'd elevated this race beyond even the Olympics. Henderson noticed my right thigh was misshapen. The quadriceps just above the knee was swollen and discolored, as if a horse had kicked it. More road damage.

It seemed almost incidental that the reason I had done all this—to gain time on McCormack—was successful. He had wilted in the heat and finished 13 minutes back. But he recovered quickly.

I wandered through a cemetery beside the road and picked pink plumeria blossoms. I got another cup from Dressendorfer and tried again. This time I brought him a specimen so clear it might have been gin. "Probably just traumatized bladder," he said. "I'll bet the pounding bruised all kinds of things."

I tried to swim, to let the little waves revive me. They rolled me about, cloudy water and bright green shreds of seaweed before my eyes, and almost drowned me. I was made to lie in the shade of a pandanus tree, on a white towel, and it seemed as if I slept, for I had the impression of having been in a lonely place for too long. But that was over, I was coming back.

There was a period when the discomfort seemed all right, justified by its origin, by my having been able to measure up to an old, hard standard. Then Scaff brought another can of beer and sat with me, impressed by my effort, admitting it was not of his world. I thought I'd get a second opinion on blood in one's urine.

"I'd say it means your system is cracking," he said. "It's a sign of impending injury."

"Great. Why hasn't this ever happened to me before?"

"You're older now, of course." He said it aggressively, with the sense of age being an equalizer, that which brings us all low. But it struck me then that this brute fact of all our lives, their being temporal, had been shown by my experience to be something not especially worrisome. If there was a lesson in these hard-racing days it was that you ran until you dropped, and then you lay under a tree with faint melodies infiltrating your consciousness and knew the rightness of everything physical having an end.

I let my mind run on where it would. It seemed, if any of this were right, that we only feel cheated of immortality when we are young and racing headlong. But when we begin to have intimations of that eventual tiredness, we may feel better. It isn't necessarily solace that age brings to bear on this question. But it is a harbinger, a foretaste. When I peacefully slipped from consciousness under that tree it was, in Updike's phrase, "death's rehearsal."

Other people sat with me, not as with the sick, but with a regard for what I'd been through because they had been through something like it. I was absolutely without self-consciousness and grateful for others being there to hear my silly jokes and homilies. Eventually, with some food and juice, I rallied. After dinner, when most of the camp began dancing happily to loud music, I sat alone on the beach and watched the sea, the flickering light of Honolulu. I was withdrawn by then and almost lamenting the loss of that beatific state of exhaustion, wishing I could be as natural in other times of life.

Then I realized the idea of self-consciousness is simply another aspect of the thought/action dichotomy. Reflection on oneself, if it is constant second-guessing, can be paralyzing. Thought has to make way for action. Even to reach out to a friend requires the stilling of the whirling computer. Just do it.

I knew then that it would be difficult to leave the really hard running. Unlike writing, that most self-conscious of arts, it is the only thing I do with abandon.

After two recovery days in Honolulu, and a look at the spectacular northwest coast of Maui from our plane, we resumed. Physically, I was nowhere near rested. At most, I was in remission. The first day's run of 15 miles on Maui began with each of my legs seeming to weight 100 pounds. The first half was uphill. I led McCormack, whose strength was more and more in the downhill.

Across the southwest flank of 10,000-foot Mt. Haleakala I broke away through hillside pastures and high stands of eucalyptus. The last miles were undulating. My sore right quadriceps worsened dramatically. I favored it, pushing only on the rises, and was lucky to win by a minute.

"The days are running out," McCormack said. Our bodies were white with the salt we had soaked up in our rest. "Margarita salt," he said. We camped on the cushiony ground of the Tedeschi Vineyards, where they make a fragrant, airy pineapple wine. They brought out ice wrapped in philodendron leaves for our legs.

McCormack had to try to take back a chunk of my 11 minutes. "Tomorrow," said Scaff, gazing at the offshore island of Kahoolawe 3,000 feet below, "is almost all downhill, and the wind will be behind. Probably hot, too. It's desert until Kaupo. We go to the church there, 19 miles."

The only thing he got right was the distance. The morning was wet and the wind blasted us right in the face. McCormack began almost desperately, shooting away on the early downhills. My leg was no better. I let him go, mentally sacrificing five minutes, hoping that I could hold him in sight when we hit sea level. But the wind and some unexpected uphills, and some hard work, let me catch him. All sense of keeping contact or of taking shelter from the wind was gone now. I would pass on a climb. On the downgrade, he'd overtake me and pull a discouraging distance ahead. But on the next ascent he would weaken, that strength of leg which once drove him through the wind draining away, and I would labor up and by. After 10 miles I crested a hill with a 100-yard lead of my own. McCormack would say later that I looked so strong that he was on the point of coasting. But while he watched, I received an arrow between the shoulder blades.

To assist my arrhythmic descents I'd been swinging my arms and shoulders too wildly. In return I'd gotten a spasm in the center of my back. I cried out and stopped, let it ease a little, and continued picking my way down.

McCormack caught up at once. "What happened?" he asked, astonished, genuinely concerned. I told him. When he passed, it was not exactly guiltily, but he looked away.

With six to go he had a quarter mile. The terrain saved me. My back held together on the uphills, which I could run correctly, and I was very careful on the downhills. We had to curl around a foaming bay, the road turning to rock and dirt and rising, always rising. I got him with three to go; he cracked, and I won by five minutes.

"It's all over," he said when he came in. "From now on I just figure to run under control, to be able to go home in one piece."

"There is too much left to say that," I insisted. His was the kind of concession I'd felt like making when he'd beaten me by a mile on our sixth day. "We don't know what will happen to us."

We had really worked ourselves into a place of isolation. The land was mountainside right into the sea, the cliffs black and green, the ocean clouded with black sand. We bathed in a stream and camped in the churchyard. Cold wind whipped at the tent. A pair of beautiful horses walked about the camp, requesting apples. I watched the gray breakers, thinking that surely McCormack had meant what he said. By all evidence he was finished. But he should resist, I thought. Resist if only for the sake of resisting. It's never over until it's over. Rather than relief at this improvement in my chances, I felt determined to run just as hard as before, to refuse his concession, to hold to the terms of the race.

We had a windfall day off. The schedule dictated a run of 20 miles to Hana, but at three miles 100 yards of road had fallen into the sea, leaving sheer, uncrossable cliff. So we made the day an untimed hike and sent scouts into the interior to find a way around. McCormack's police whistle signaled success. We helped each other up the slope and across a ridge and down, along hastily strung ropes, through a 20-foot chimney to the road. Then in congenial groups we walked the rest of the way, past waterfalls and newborn foals and into rain forest.

We passed the green promontory where Charles Lindbergh lies, and finally, being ridiculously tired by now, because this walking business was killing, we were rescued by the vans, which had gone almost all the way around the island. They took us to camp at lovely Wainapanapa Bay, and everyone was happy.

The next morning we ran 16 miles along the famously curvy road from Hana, finding the rise and fall to be far more memorable than the curves. Krichko, out of contention but feeling good, got away. A three-mile downhill into Keanae seemed calculated to batter legs. I eased, but not enough. I had twinges up and down both calves. Yet McCormack finished 10 minutes behind me. A man of his word. I now had a 27-minute lead with four days to go.

The next day would be 20.7 miles. Then we'd finish with legs of 10, 14 and 10 miles. The thing to do was dog the long one and save something for the last three. Trotting around before the start I had wrong feelings in the left hip and both calves, morning twinges.

McCormack and Krichko set a solid pace. It was wet and cool. McCormack wore his cap that said F.D.N.Y.—THE BRAVEST. As the group strung out, Rick Landau, of New York said, "Every day it's the same. The same people ahead, the same order."

I got warm and ran in third, trying to relax and banish the nagging worry that filled me whenever McCormack was ahead. The road's pattern was constant, uphill to the crest of one of the great green headlands that jut into the Pacific on Maui's north shore, then down into a new valley, across the stream at its back, then up and out, to the next crest and the sight of a new valley, the runners ahead already climbing out of it.

Within three miles my right calf was catching, first on the uphill when it had to stretch, soon on the downhill. On a rough patch the calf went with a jolt, making me leap and call out, startling birds from the forest. I kept on, emotionally charged, understanding that my shouting when the pain speared the leg was a sign that the last reserves had come forth. This was an echo of the Olympic marathon in 1972, in which I'd gone from second place to fourth in the last five miles, losing a medal. It had been a cramp in my leg then, too.

By the second aid station I was down to hobbling nine-or-10 minute miles. McCormack would need only 10 miles to take all of my 27 minutes.

Our field began to pass. Bob Holtel, a track coach from Manhattan Beach, Calif., said, "Now I know there is injustice in the world."

He was gone before that registered. "No," I said to the cliffs, "this is the playing out of natural law."

Dick Smith, of Eugene, passed and said, "Think of next week, next month. Don't hurt yourself."

"I won't." I said. But I knew I would.

At the 10-mile aid station, Russell Wilbur, a large and tender Hawaiian who was one of the support staff, gave me a Coke. I told him it looked like I was going to have to walk. I had never done that in a race before.

"But," he said, "you are not going to quit."

I shook my head, and I walked.

It was like slowing down had been, a temporary relief. Soon the calf was in constant cramp, from the back of the knee to the Achilles tendon. It was hard to limp uphill. Most of the field had passed. The sun came out.

I timed myself between mileposts. Eighteen minutes. Three and a third miles an hour. At that rate, I'd be done in about five hours. At 12 miles, Dr. Harry Hlavac, our podiatrist, who had passed earlier, was at an aid station. He'd rummaged through people's belongings, but had found only a roll of electrician's tape. I sat on a cooler and he iced my calf, dried it, wrapped it with that sticky, black friction tape and put an Ace bandage around it all. "Might help," he said a bit dubiously.

I went on. It was a little better. The tight wrap kept me from stretching to the point where it seized.

There was a lot of thought in there, to fill the sour hollow of a race now lost. I felt more alone than when running, yanked out of my familiar element. I wished for a friend left at home. I lectured myself for that. Why have two people suffer instead of one? But I still wished for her.

The basic lesson presented itself with every step. I'd judged all the elements, the distance, the resilience of my legs, the hills, the pace, the heat, the competition. And I'd made a mistake. Somewhere back there, on the prideful day before the rest interval, or in whipping McCormack over the last three miles of the run to Kaupo Church, or in not easing along with him yesterday, the day I'd had calf twinges; I'd done too much. "That's easy to accept," I said aloud. "It's the pain of the consequences that's all out of proportion."

But it wasn't easy to accept, in part because it wasn't the infirm body that lost the race. That had proved itself worthy of victory. It was the infirm mind making the adolescent athlete's mistake, letting wishful thinking replace the conclusions gained through 23 years of observation. I had made a greedy mistake, overstepping known bounds, and the punishment was somehow inevitably, naturally steep. This had been Sisyphus' sin, too. Later I looked it up to be sure. After he died, he'd won permission from Pluto to return temporarily to earth from the underworld, to chastise his wife. But when he was on earth again, he loved it so much he refused to go back. "Many years more he lived facing the curve of the gulf, the sparkling sea." wrote Camus in his classic essay on the myth. Finally Mercury came and forced him into the underworld, where his rock awaited: "the price that must be paid for the passions of this earth."

And that price is the greater for one's being fully conscious of it. I seemed a literal Sisyphus for a time, temporarily done straining. I recalled, almost involuntarily, splendid races and bad ones, but nothing like this. "This really is a comedown," I thought. For a while I was cold. "A face that toils so close to stones is already stone itself," Camus continued. "When the call of happiness become too insistent, it happens that melancholy rises in man's heart. This is the rock's victory. This is the rock." All we can offer in opposition is our will. We decide how to react to our punishment.

There were still one or two people behind me, our pure walkers, our injured-for-the-duration. I thought of them. They did this every day. There are different worlds. I thought of special Olympians, of wheelchair marathoners, of the choices of a man like Terry Fox. And I realized, slowly, grudgingly, that I'd been spoiled by a life of strength. There is nothing inherently horrible about walking 13 miles on a sunny day in Hawaii, even with a sore leg. It was simply the wrenching transition from running well that saddened me. Accepting that, I was not uplifted, but the worst was over.

The land changed, the jungly hills giving way to cane and pineapple. With a mile to go, Don Zaph and Slick Chapman brought me a Coke. They explained every few hundred yards that there wasn't far to go.

We mounted a hill and saw a crowd of tanned people ahead. I walked in, making a show of stopping my watch. (4:55:01). Mc-Cormack was there, and we hung on to each other. He had to walk on the uphills the last five miles. "You were the smart one." I said.

"It takes the satisfaction out of it to have it happen like this," he said. But we both knew it could happen no other way. Later, it occurred to me that he had won the race by conceding the race.

The last three days seemed to loom as a new career in walking, but the calf, diagnosed by Hlavac to have strains and tears all along the medial part of the gastrocnemius, improved considerably, and I was able to cover most of the distance in a sort of hunched trot, though I fell to fifth place overall. We rode a catamaran back to Honolulu from Lahaina, the flying fish skittering in the sun, porpoises escorting us past Diamond Head.

There was a party and an award ceremony that night at the Scaffs' home. McCormack accepted his trophy rather gravely, saying, "It was a bittersweet experience. Sure, I knew it would be run so hard that we'd cripple everyone, I made it that way, and that's the way it worked out. But on the day we hiked to Hana, I saw that there was more to it than white lines on a black road." He swallowed hard. "I'll never do this again, this way. Next time I'll try to take a part of each of the others into me, to know what they experience."

His seemed a natural and good reaction, the effort, damage and narrowness of the race producing an affirmation of a broader life. His was the traditionally mature response, the leaving of competition for richer relationships.

Mine was not. "Would you run it hard again?" was Scaff's question.

"Probably," I said, almost embarrassed to admit it to him. But as the weeks passed and my legs came back and I set down this account, I grew less shy about it. I'll run it hard. I know more about Maui hills now. And more about me. I am still not rid of Sisyphus' sin. And I'm not too sure McCormack is either.

ROAD WARRIORS

Hal Higdon

Early in the Trans-Indiana Run, I found myself in step with my friend Conn Day, chatting about inconsequential items —dogs we had encountered, the height of corn by the side of the road—anything to divert our minds from the enormity of our enterprise, which was to run from one end of the state of Indiana to the other, a distance of 350 miles, in 10 days. "What do we tell people when they ask us why we're doing this?" worried Conn.

That was a question to which I had given considerable thought, knowing that mountain-climber Bill Mallory's time-honored palliative, "Because it's there" doesn't quite work for ultramarathoning. Eventually I decided upon a proper response, which I offered to Conn:

"Because it seemed like a neat thing to do."

Days later, 235 miles behind us but 115 still to go, I stumbled into a Lafayette restaurant and encountered Lora Cartwright, a Purdue graduate who still holds the age-14 marathon record. The backs of my legs were painfully sunburned from too much noonday sun. My right ankle was puffed like a balloon with some yet-to-be-diagnosed injury. I had come to the restaurant to eat not because I was hungry, but for a purely technical reason: I had to get some food in my stomach before I fell asleep simply in order to survive the next day.

Lora asked the obvious question and I responded with the prepared response. She looked at me for a moment and smiled with the wisdom of one who also has run many miles: "Does it still seem like a neat thing to do?"

Well, no, but I knew that once the miles were covered and our wounds healed, the ten of us who had chosen to run from Indiana's southernmost to northernmost border, the Ohio River to Lake Michigan—from river to shining lake, so to speak—would look back on our accomplishment with a perverse pleasure. As Doc Henry put it, "This run is like the Army: You wish you hadn't joined, but you wouldn't want to have missed the experience."

Running the length of Indiana was not an idea that had blossomed overnight. Steve Kearney and I had discussed the possibility of a Trans-Indiana Run as long as 15 years ago. Steve, a Ball State graduate, taught math at Chesterton High School, near my home in Michigan City, Indiana. In the early 1970s, Steve and I once had examined maps and plotted several routes, figuring we could cover the state in a week or so. Whether common sense or inertia intervened, we never did the run and our plans withered until one summer at the Olympic track trials. One day at the Coliseum, fellow journalist Don Kardong mentioned a project for which he had been hired as consultant: the filming of the Bunion Derby novel, "Ryan's Run." I told Don of my unfulfilled dream of running Indiana. That started me thinking.

Home from the trials, I began examining maps, an act that did not escape the attention of my wife Rose. Soon after, we visited Steve and Martha Kearney with a present for their new baby. Steve had just staggered in from a hot 13-miler and sat crumpled on the sofa, shirt soaked with sweat, eyes glazed, barely responding to our conversation, until Rose said, "Hal's gone crazy again. I caught him studying a Rand McNally road atlas with a magnifying glass."

This caught Steve's attention. "All right," he said.

"We're going!" Although we hadn't discussed our dream in years, Steve knew instantly the reason for my madness. The Trans-Indiana Run was on.

ॐ

Looking back, the most pleasurable part about Trans-Indiana was the planning, the year of effort related to logistics: Which route? How far each day? What motel each night? I loved visiting county courthouses on town squares with Civil War monuments on the lawns, talking to old folk behind dusty desks, collecting multi-colored maps, which usually cost 50 cents. A bargain. Sliding a ruler across an Indiana map, we determined that if we ran along the western border with Illinois, the distance was only 270 miles. But that would put us on heavily-traveled highways, which I wanted to avoid both for safety and aesthetic reasons. A friend with the state highway department helped select a 300-mile route using roads for which the traffic count was less than 2,000 vehicles a day, barely a car a minute.

Even that was more traffic than I desired, and eventually we chose roads with names like 600W or 1,000N. So successful were we in route selection that several times during the run we would go two hours without being passed by a car. One of our group counted five cars during another five-hour period.

But solitude bore a burden. Such low-traffic roads inevitably were hillier and more circuitous than better-traveled highways. Many were gravel. On one remote road, we would even need to ford a stream because there was no bridge. During a springtime reconnaissance, Steve reported that all our preliminary mileage estimates were low, that we would cover close to 350 miles. Blame also my desire to start in Owensboro, Kentucky, about as far south as the Ohio River dips in its meandering route along the lower border of Indiana. Owensboro had special significance: my father had been born there. We would finish in Michiana Shores on Indiana's Michigan border, only a mile from where Rose and I raised our three children. So Trans-Indiana became, for me, a rite of passage.

Others would need to find their own excuses. Not wishing to waste all the planning on ourselves, Steve and I leaked word of Trans-Indiana via the monthly, *Ultrarunning.* I received numerous inquiries, but most seemed put off by my insistence that this was a run, not a race. "No bugles, no drums, no trophies, no T-shirts," I warned inquirers. And little support. I could have sought sponsors, or tried to involve a charity, but I didn't want to make the run into something bigger than it was. Others had run farther, or faster— or farther *and* faster. I wasn't trying to compete with them; I simply wanted to run the length of my home state, whose license plates bear the motto: WANDER INDIANA. And that seemed like a neat thing to do.

Day One

Friday, July 11. Ten runners appear in Owensboro. Half that number, including Steve and myself, are members of our local Dunes Running Club. Rich Breiner of Michigan City teaches at Purdue North Central. Conn Day, at age 26 the youngest, works as a truck driver for a produce company in LaPorte. Dr. Howard Henry, at age 64 the oldest, is a general practitioner from Knox. Richard M. Hearns, Sr. and Jr., come from Kinnelon, New Jersey and Greensboro, North Carolina, respectively. Senior works for an insurance company; Junior is a cost accountant. Michael Schreiber, who lives in Mexico, is an anthropologist turned author, including among his books, *The Art of Running.* Bill Mack is a junior high school principal from Defiance, Ohio. Dave Kanners of Rochester, Michigan has the most intriguing background. Owner of an auto repair shop, Dave once competed as a drag racer, having won a National Hot Rod Association championship. His wife Sue is biking along, as is Rose.

All starters have ultramarathoning experience, although mine is limited to a single 50K race. Each of the first eight days in Trans-Indiana will be longer than the longest run I ever had made in my life! Nevertheless, I anticipate no problems—as long as I run slow enough. I hope to average 10:00 miles, despite suggestions by ultramarathoning friends that I could run faster. "This is a run, not a race," I keep reminding them as well as myself.

To dampen any tendency toward enthusiasm, I opt to walk the

first 10 minutes after our pre-dawn start in Owensboro. That takes me to the middle of the suspension bridge spanning the Ohio River. The waters below seem still in the near darkness; a barge upstream moves with the current, its searchlight swinging rhythmically from bank to bank. As I begin to jog on the bridge's down slope, I can see Steve far ahead, running with Dave on a gravel road that follows the river bank.

Originally we had planned to start on the Indiana side of the river, but when I saw how close our hotel, the Executive Inn, was to the bridge, I suggested we start from the hotel. "It's only a couple of extra miles," I say. Those words would return to haunt me.

Everyone carries hand-drawn maps, a necessity since we have insufficient manpower to monitor turns. Each evening, we will meet for a briefing on the next day's course. Not everyone would pay attention, however, and one of the worst offenders would be Rich. In the first mile, Rich starts to run under the bridge—the only one across the Ohio for 30 miles in either direction—when he looks up and sees runners going across it. "It suddenly dawned on me that I should be up there instead of down here," he admits later.

My early strategy is to run solo rather than risk someone else's too-fast pace. I have just purchased a new plastic wristwatch that beeps every 10 minutes, alerting me to walk and drink from a fanny-pack canteen. Every other beep, I eat a granola bar. Even moving at such a methodical pace, I catch and pass all but Dave and Steve in the first few miles. We are all running nervous, fearful of what might happen when the sun, now peeking through the cornstalks, rises higher in the cloudless sky. Sweat pours off us because of high humidity. The temperature is on its way into the 90s.

At 14 miles I stop at our only support vehicle, a rented camper driven by Pat Barbus, a member of Steve's track team. Retrieving a camera from the camper, I snap others as they approach. I hope to record our journey on film, although as it turns out, this is the last time I have either the energy or the desire to take a photograph. I drink amply, refilled my canteen, and continue. With the gravel behind us, Rose and Sue are now cycling, providing moral support as well as occasional sips from the canteens they carry on their bikes.

I run with Rich and Conn, one or the other surging ahead as we alternately run and walk, each still fearful of accepting another's pace. At about standard marathon distance, I begin to wilt and they drift ahead. At one corner Rose recruits two young girls at a farmhouse to direct following runners to turn left. She thanks them for their help, which includes fresh water. "This is the most exciting thing that's happened this summer," the girls gush.

Somehow the 38 anticipated first-day miles have stretched to 42. I walk most of the final ones, regretting my jaunty decision to begin over the bridge. I have been nearly eight hours on the road, my goal of 10:00 miles and pre-noon finishes already shattered. With the camper and our day's finish point in sight, I look over my shoulder and see Michael a quarter mile behind, jogging.

"This is a run, not a race," I remind myself. Nevertheless I begin to jog to keep him behind me. We climb in the camper to be driven to our motel in Huntingburg. Everyone finishes, although Bill Mack took a wrong turn, ran past the finish point and calls to be picked up at a bar. "They have cold beer," Bill says. "Don't hurry."

Day Two

I've known Conn Day maybe a half dozen years and, though likable and basically friendly, he is one of the shyest individuals I've ever met, rarely offering more than wisps of conversation. Now, on Day Two, running in his company for 20 or 30 miles, I discover an entirely new dimension to Conn's personality: He suddenly becomes a gifted conversationalist. As we run through a long, flat stretch, nothing but cornstalks in all directions, Conn recalls his first marathon in DeKalb, Illinois on an equally flat, double-loop course: "The winner ran 2:51 and I ran 3:38—and I could see him all the way!"

We pass a rural cemetery, many of its gravestones decorated with fresh flowers. Conn notes: "Cemeteries always are on the highest ground. That's to give people a head start to heaven." Before taking up running Conn used to race motorcycles, but says he got tired of riding home in a vehicle different from the one he came in. Meaning one with a siren. He was delighted to find that hitting the wall in a marathon was a metaphorical, not a medical, event.

No longer content to run solo, we now huddle together for support. Dave and Rich are somewhere out ahead forging a fast pace. The Hearns cruise gently behind along with Bill and Doc Henry. Conn paces Steve and I with his plastic wristwatch, which he sets to beep every two minutes. We run four minutes, walk two. Later, we go two-two, although that seems harder. The first pattern reminds me of doing half-mile intervals on the track, the second, quarter-miles. But it gets me through the day. With five miles to go out of 40, I tell myself that a half dozen more track intervals and I

can walk the last few miles into Loogootee, our second-day destination. But on the edge of town, I feel my body temperature soar.
We have been on the road nearly eight hours again, temperatures
higher than yesterday. If I have heat stroke, I hope it happens atop
a high hill. I douse myself with hoses kindly offered by townspeo-
ple, then stop at a Dairy Queen to down a milk shake before walking the last mile to our motel.

Dave and Rich have preceded us, despite taking a wrong turn
and running south before realizing the sun was on their left instead
of right. The ranks of those going the full distance has begun to
thin. Michael rode in the camper today all day and would the next
day too. Bill finishes with a foot cramped from tendinitis, may not
be able to continue. Doc Henry decides that, considering the stress
of the first two days, he will rest the third. Later that afternoon, we
visit a nearby lake and my left leg cramps badly when I attempt to
swim. No permanent damage, but I am fearful for tomorrow, pro-
jected at 48 miles. All of our distance estimates thus far have been
low. When I ask Steve about tomorrow's actual mileage, he replies:
"You don't want to know."

Day Three

Everyone desires an early departure, so I bang on doors at 3:30
A.M. and immediately leave, walking into darkness a half hour before the group's scheduled start. My strategy is: walk until someone catches me and only then run. I hope to sneak in six or eight
walking miles, but after three Steve comes upon me. The coward:
He dressed quickly after my knock and immediately gave chase.

We go nine before Dave and Rich appear, and all stop to sit on the steps of a general store in Raglesville, sipping soft drinks from a machine. Nary a soul stirs in town, although the Hearns, arriving later, encounter an Amish family going to church by horse and buggy. Dave and Rich depart at a pace neither Steve nor I desire to match. Soon Conn appears behind. He started late while treating a blister and has had to work hard to catch up. Conn seems more than willing to move at our gentler pace. We stop when we see the camper and I sit on its stoop, not certain whether I can go the full distance. Steve offers to carry my canteen and begins to leave. "I'm starting slow," he says, figuring we'll soon catch him—but that's the last we see Steve that day. Conn and I no longer run his watch, we run the territory: walking uphills, running downhills. Soon I am reduced to walking downhills as well. Trans-Indiana has become a mind-altering experience for me. Earlier in the summer, Marvin Skagerberg and Malcolm Campbell passed through Michigan City on a transcontinental race. I breakfasted with them and handler Nick Marshall, seeing the pair start that morning and thinking their 10:00 pace "slowish." Now 15:00 miles seem "fast." Several years ago, Rose ran Honolulu, her first and only marathon. Her time was 6:32. After being on the road seven hours, it occurs to me that, matched against Rose's performance, I would be trailing her. Instant humility. I inform Conn I plan to stop in Bloomfield, 29 miles. He does the same. Riding in the camper to McCormick State Park, our evening destination, I feel defeated. Cumulative fatigue over three hot days, more than today's long run, had halted me. With our early starts, I don't seem to be getting enough sleep, or enough food. Eating becomes an ordeal when you're exhausted. At McCormick's Canyon Inn I down three bowls of soup before going to bed. Arising, I encounter Conn in the hall-way. "Well?" I ask. "Well," he says. We decide to return to the course and continue the job.

Jerry Jacobs, a cyclist from LaPorte who came to help over the weekend, agrees to drive us back to Bloomfield. We stop at a Mc-Donald's in Spencer for hamburgers, fries, and shakes, our training meal. At 5:30 P.M. in the town square, a bank clock indicates the temperature is 96 degrees in the shade. Steve earlier had spotted a thermometer registering 110 degrees: "It was in the sun, but so was I."

We first walk in deference to our recent meal as much as the heat, but run as the sun moves closer to the horizon. Running be-comes pleasant again along a winding road with overhanging trees and long views over valleys cut by the White River. After three hours of running, darkness more than fatigue forces me to stop at a town called, ironically, New Hope. Dave and Rich also had stopped there earlier in the day. Steve had gone a mile further to Pottersville, matched by Conn. The Hearns went only to Bloom-field.

Day Four

Day Four to Greencastle offers an "easy" 31-miler, so Dave, Rich, Steve, Conn and I attempt to play catch-up, returning to our stop points. Doc Henry and the Hearns, however, start in Spencer along with Michael, running again. Only Bill remains injured, but thoughtfully assists Pat in the camper. Every day someone has got-ten lost, so we locate some old bed sheets at our motel and rip them into strips to tie on poles and bushes at critical turns. This helps prevent people wandering off course, though not entirely. "Everyone's spaced out," notes Rose. After sleeping fitfully, I begin the day's run fatigued and nauseated. After Dave and Rich speed off, I find myself running solo, then walking solo, then lying under a tree trying to remember whose dumb idea this whole thing was. A glass of cider offered by a farmer's wife revives me, but when Rose and Sue appear in Jerry's car, I leap for the back seat. I've gone only 20 miles. "I'll finish this stage later," I promise. "Later?" worries Rose.

"Like November."

I still refuse to surrender entirely and decide that part of my problem is insufficient nutrition. I haven't taken time to eat enough. After several days munching granola bars, I no longer can stand their dryness. Too many carbonated drinks have begun to make me sick. Steve and I find a Pizza Hut near the DePauw University campus where we're staying and order spaghetti, garlic bread, and salad, washed down with a couple of glasses of beer. After a nap, the group heads for Noble Roman Pizza for more of the same. Two spaghetti meals in one day seems overkill, but Rich is ahead of me. When we walk into Noble Roman, a waitress says, stunned, "You again?" It is Rich's third visit.

Day Five

To survive, obviously I must lower my goals. Long forgotten is my expectation to run 10:00 pace and finish each day by noon. I have not achieved that even once! I decide to run with the Hearns, Sr. and Jr., who affectionately call each other "Road Toad." Their marathon bests are 3:20 and 3:21. They finish last every day, but except for the third day debacle, the Toads do finish. At briefings, I notice that Toad Sr. pays close attention, takes precise notes, carefully copies maps, and while faster runners go astray, he and Toad Jr. happily plod their way along the correct path.

The Road Toads and I leave at 4:30 along with Michael and Doc Henry. They alternate jogging and walking, never pressing the pace, running the territory, using even the slightest upward incline as an excuse to walk, shifting back to a shuffling jog on declines. They seem to sense road shifts as delicate as half a degree.

The Toads also chatter continuously. By the time we reach the town of Bainbridge, I have received a detailed description of every marathon in the states of New Jersey and North Carolina. We grab soft drinks from a machine, but soon are caught by Doc Henry and Michael. They had run faster to Bainbridge, but stopped at a diner for breakfast. Michael, beard dripping sweat, aggressively plunges ahead and soon is out of sight, but Doc Henry stays with the Toads and myself.

If the Toads know East Coast marathons, Doc knows Indiana basketball, his memories triggered by each town we pass.

"Jeff Blue was Bainbridge's best player," recalls Doc.

"The Menke brothers played for Huntingburg. Took 'em to the state finals." That was back in the '30s.

A 4:14 miler, Doc ran track in that same era for coach Billy Hayes at Indiana University. His teammates included Roy Cochran and Fred Wilt. They participated in exercise tests by physiologist Sid Robinson, who invited them back for a retest 20 years later. "I played a lot of golf and prided myself on being in shape," says Doc, "and I tested worst of the group." Pride stung, Doc started jogging and soon discovered the Boston Marathon. "Ten years later Sid tested us again and I tested best—better even than Wilt!"

Rather than run his watch like Conn, or the territory like the Toads, Doc runs telephone poles. He runs from one telephone pole to the next—about 100 meters—then walks to the one after that. I follow this routine into the town of Ladoga, but eventually find the constant stop-start oppressive and shift to longer runs and walks, still staying near Doc. The Toads have remained with us, but when I look around outside Ladoga they have slowed. Moving up are Dave and Rich, who started later, and remarkably have not yet gotten lost. Maybe that's because accompanying them today is Joe Kenny, a medical intern from Indianapolis who joined us for today's stage, one of the pleasanter ones. I am tempted to go with their faster pace, but decide to remain with Doc. On the outskirts of Crawfordsville, however, I spot a Dairy Queen and halt. Anything to cut the journey by even a mile.

Rich arrives at the General Lew Wallace Motor Inn and finds that Michael has preceded him. "I guess I won the lap prize today," boasts Michael. When Rich points out the difference in their starting times, Michael growls: "Nobody was chaining you to the bed at 4:00 this morning."

Our group, understandably, has developed a close rapport during our long journey. Only Michael, who mostly dines and runs alone, remains aloof. Dinner that evening deteriorates into a joke-telling session, Doc Henry offering the worst one about a man who gets into an accident and is informed by a doctor after an operation that there is good news and bad news. Told the bad news first, he learns they had to amputate his leg. "What's the good news?" asks the man.

The doctor replies: "We sold your shoe."

Day Six

Today we're headed for Lafayette, over mostly flat farmland and gravel roads. We have been blessed by cool weather the last few days: mid-80s. Everybody leaves early except Steve and me. He had wanted to stay up late to watch the All-Star baseball game, so we go at 6:30, an hour after dawn. I welcome the extra rest a late start offers. Rose bikes with us.

Halfway through the 34-mile stage, we stop at a farmhouse for water. "What is this," asks the farmer, "a run for crippled children?"

"No," I respond, puzzled.

The farmer continues: "I saw some crippled guy limp through here. Had a pole and his knee was bandaged."

When we arrive in Lafayette—late after taking a wrong turn—we realize the farmer had been talking about Dave. He had come into my room late the night before, worried about a swollen ankle. I recommended ice and aspirin: ". . . and call me at the office tomorrow." Soon after we arrived at the Howard Johnson's motel, Dave limps into the lobby using a broken branch for a staff, T-shirt wrapped around his leg. He removes one shoe, revealing a foot swollen worse than it was last night. I console him: "The good news is we sold your shoe."

I have little reason to laugh. My right ankle also is badly swollen. I join the ice-and-aspirin club.

Day Seven

When I knock on Dave's door ready to begin Day Seven at dawn, Sue answers. Dave is but a motionless blob in bed, hidden beneath the blanket. Sue says Dave cannot continue.

Everyone else is running, however, including Bill, who went half the distance yesterday. Except for Steve and I, everyone left at 3:30, two hours ahead. To cut some of their lead, we take a diagonal shortcut along railroad tracks. Nothing in the Trans-Indiana rules (which I invent as we go along) says we can't do this.

The shortcut helps us reach Battleground, 10 miles, in 80 minutes. Nevertheless, I am surprised to see five runners ahead on the road. My first reaction is that it must be the Battleground cross-country team, but it is our group. They turned left where they should have turned right and wandered in circles, eventually finding their way back on course via the interstate. "We knew we were in trouble," said Doc Henry, "when after two hours we saw a sign saying 'Howard Johnson's, one mile.'" The Road Toads, running on their own, tortoises vs. hares, made the proper turn and are far ahead.

Fast running seems to suit me better than the slow running of previous days, so I push to pass the Toads. Steve fades, troubled by sore Achilles tendons. Only Rich catches me when I pause to don tights and a long-sleeved shirt as protection against the relentless sun. Stopping in Monticello for a milk shake with three miles remaining to our destination, Indiana Beach, I realize that this is the first day that I have averaged better than 10:00 pace. I also will finish before noon.

Day Eight

Our Road Warriors have begun to show signs of rust. Dave and Bill, injured, have left for home; Michael also departs. Steve's tendons and my ankle are swollen. Conn's shins ache. Rich is tired of getting lost and wants to run from behind rather than in front. We decide to start early and start slow. At the briefing, Richard Hearn, Sr. says almost wistfully, "I hate to think that this elite group is reduced to the pace of the Road Toads."

Actually I am reduced to less than that, deciding to walk the 36-mile stage with Steve, hoping this will provide a day's rest to permit me to run well during the final two stages, short runs of only 20 and 25 miles.

Unfortunately, it's a poor strategy since eight hours of walking fatigues me more than running might have. Every muscle in my body throbs, the way you feel when you have the flu. I try my first running steps in the 29th mile, but can't get even to the next telephone pole. Frank and Karen Hutchinson have driven down from Michigan City to offer support. I finish the last miles into North Judson in their pickup truck. Somehow I don't even feel embarrassed.

Day Nine

Ice-and-aspirin fail to contain my swelling ankle, which seems to bother me less when I run fast. For my Day Nine strategy, I decide to race Rich. I also know another railroad-track shortcut that will cut a mile from our distance. Once off the tracks, Rich and I begin pushing the pace to what I judge is faster than seven-minute miles. We are now in Dunes Running Club territory and members come to provide support, liquids every mile if we want it. It's easier to run when you don't need to pack your own water.

After a dozen miles, Rich surges ahead, but my strategy has

worked. My ankle feels good and I'm far enough along so that I will finish early again, important only that it will provide more time to rest and eat for tomorrow.

In the closing miles I find myself catching Conn and Doc Henry, who started an hour before. Doc is running telephone poles again. I figure I'll run in with them. I come to within a telephone pole-length of the pair. As they stop to walk, I stop to walk, expecting to catch them on the next run. But Doc looks over his shoulder, sees me, and starts to run early. No longer interested in racing, I walk the last mile to our stopping point at South Central High School.

Day Ten

My son Kevin, just back from a European honeymoon, decides to pace me through Day Ten. Several club members also appear: Jeff Samelson, Mary Taylor. My ankle is no better or worse than before, and I run comfortably ahead of even Rich, who seems content to go slow this last day. But coming down an incline I feel a twinge that causes me to slow. Leg hurting, I am reduced again to survival pace—walking, jogging, grasping for drinks. Ten days to Trans-Indiana, and I have hit the wall on every one of them.

Then with a half dozen miles remaining, I suddenly find a rhythm that causes the pain in my leg to subside. I accelerate and feel better rather than worse. I catch several early-starters, including Doc Henry. I wave going past. In the last two miles there's a shortcut across a railroad trestle that will save everybody a half-mile detour. I nearly stumble to my knees crossing it, but resume a fast pace again. A glance at my watch tells me I'll finish just under four hours for about-marathon distance. That's far from my PR, but I feel proud of this accomplishment.

Just before the finish in Michiana Shores there's one last hill, a dune actually, and from the top of it I look out across Lake Michigan, glistening with reflected sunlight, boats rocking on its surface, bathers peppering the beach. Club members and earlier finishers stand below cheering my approach. Coming down the final incline, I raise one fist to salute them and sit on a bench above the beach before taking off my shoes to enter the water. My longest run is done. Rose has a bottle of champagne and pops the cork. I raise my glass, but can't think of a toast. A woman in a bathing suit appears from the beach. "Is there a run today?" she inquires.

I say yes, and she wants to know where it began. "Owensboro, Kentucky," I reply.

The woman laughs, then the truth begins sinking in. Her jaw drops. "You're serious, aren't you?"

I smile: "It seemed like a neat thing to do."

Epilogue

Monday afternoon I sit in the office of my friendly, neighborhood podiatrist, Mann Spitler, who has just clipped two X-ray negatives to a glass box. He points to a bulging area midway up my right tibia where I have a stress fracture. "No running for the next four weeks," says Dr. Spitler. I take the news calmly, since I figure I've done enough running in the last 10 days to last me at least that long. I'll swim, cycle, lift weights and survive to run again.

I have failed to run the full length of Indiana—missing 20 miles near Greencastle, another seven at North Judson—but somehow it no longer bothers me. Maybe it's acceptable to leave a few miles in my life untrod.

Several days later I receive a letter from a runner who originally planned to join us. After being accepted into the Western States 100, however, he decided to run that event instead. But he wanted to know the results of Trans-Indiana and said he may run it next time.

I respond that since Trans-Indiana was a run not a race, there are no "results." As keeper of the rule book, I decreed that all seven who made it to Michiana the final day tied for first. Tied for second were our three dropouts, who gave their best. We timed the race with a calendar rather than a stopwatch; the shared record stands at 10 days. As for the next Trans-Indiana Run, participants decided that it should become a centennial rather than an annual affair. I told him to put the year 2085 in his date book.

WINGS OF ICARUS

Ed Ayres

The earth never tires,
The earth is rude, silent, incomprehensible at first,
Nature is incomprehensible at first,
Be not discouraged, keep on, there are divine
things well envelop'd . . .
—Walt Whitman

Two nights before the start of the Western States 100 Mile Run, Sharon woke up suddenly to an incongruous sound: a high, steady roar she thought she recognized from the years when we lived in a cramped apartment above the *Running Times* office, almost in the shadow of an interstate highway.

"Traffic!" she exclaimed with great surprise and disappointment. We were staying in a rented ski condo surrounded by a wall of mountains in the Sierra Nevada. There couldn't possibly be any traffic in this remote place on a June night. I poked my head out the door. It sounded like the roar of trucks. "Maybe it's the wind," I said doubtfully, but I knew it wasn't. It would take a hurricane to make a noise like that.

When we had arrived that afternoon, the first thing I had done was to go out for a run—to see what it was like to run at 7,000 foot altitude. As we had driven our rented car up the long winding road, I had experienced a familiar urge. Anytime I see a pretty meadow on the side of a mountain, I want to run on it. My relationship with grassy hillsides is as predictable as that of a dog with fire hydrants; there is an irresistible pull. Once when I was a teacher traveling with a group of students in Europe, we drove up into the Swiss Alps and the urge struck me so forcefully I had to stop the car, jump out, and run straight up the side of an Alpine hill, leaving my bewildered passengers abandoned by the roadside for 45 minutes.

Appropriately, the place we stayed the two nights before Western States was called Alpine Meadows. It was just a few miles from the more famous Squaw Valley, where the race would start, but was higher and more secluded. As we approached, I was entranced by the sight of snow on the mountainside just a few hundred yards up from the road. The air temperature was a pleasant 70. Below the snowfield, a grassy ski slope beckoned. As soon as we checked in, I jumped into my shorts and ran up the slope. It was the most perfect summer day possible. The sky was deep blue and cloudless for a thousand miles. Wildflowers grew everywhere. I ran to the point where the snow began, then dashed back to my wife and child bearing a bouquet in one hand, a snowball in the other. That night, for all the roar, there wasn't a breath of breeze coming in the open window of our bedroom.

The next morning, we went for a last pre-race jog and found the source of the noise: a great rush of water pouring off the mountain, providing at least some answer to my puzzlement about the phenomenon of vast snowfields sitting under a hot sun. The runoff sounded indeed like the rush of 18-wheelers, and maybe that trick of perception should have been a warning to me about what I was to experience in the following 24 hours. For those of us who live in the suburbs and cities, it's an easy mistake to trivialize nature—to try to explain the larger forces of the universe in terms of our own limited experience. It is the kind of mistake that would come to haunt me later.

Twenty years ago, when I was training for my first marathon, there were perhaps a thousand marathoners active in the U.S., and I suspect every one of us got accustomed to hearing oblique jokes about being "crazy" for running races of 26 miles. I think most Americans felt a bit uncomfortable with people who went to such extremes. Clinical psychologists seemed to take the view that every major deviation from normal behavior could be explained in terms of some weakness of character or misfortune of family history. If Gunther Gebel-Williams devoted his life to training tigers and elephants, no doubt it was because he was desperately unhappy in his relations with people. When Sir Edmund-Hillary felt compelled to climb the frigid heights of Everest, it was probably because he could not accept the warmth of the hearth; to believe he climbed the mountain "because it is there" was romantically naive. So, those of us who spent long hours training on the roads were no doubt running away from something.

As marathoning became more popular in the 70s, the "crazy" epithet gradually fell out of fashion. It became OK to spend two hours a day running, without it being generally supposed that what you were trying to do was to fill some empty hole in your life. My former therapist, Jim Hall, who years earlier might have urged me to confront my craziness, got so hooked on running himself that he asked me to coach him through his first marathon. We went up to Boston in 1970, and he got the thrill of his life, finishing in about four hours. I don't think even then that he thought this running stuff was quite normal, but it was a kind of craziness that was *OK*. This was around the time the book *I'm OK, You're OK* was very popular, and maybe it was a growing notion among thinking people that a *little* nuttiness is not such a bad thing, as long as it isn't taken to unhealthy extremes. Jim would probably have felt better about me if I'd stuck with marathons, but by then my restless soul was already exploring the lure of ultras.

It was in the summer of 1985 that I made the decision to run the Western States 100 Miles. At the time I was going through a period of great personal strife, and I saw this extraordinary event as a means of setting things right. For me, this would be no lighthearted frolic in the wilderness, no middle-aged reliving of Boy Scout adventures. It was a wild gamble against impossible odds. In the movies, such gambles pay off. In real life they don't. And I wasn't under any illusion that the Western States 100 is anything *but* real life.

But that's my point. Whatever other madness it was, this venture was not an escape; it was a deliberate confrontation. From the moment I sent in my $125 entry fee, I knew I was committed to an experience that would bring me eyeball to eyeball with certain truths that are very easy to avoid in the rush of normal life. On the trail of the Western States Endurance Run, life is reduced to its most naked fundamentals. It's interesting that non-runners seem to assume that when a runner hits the trail and leaves all the work of daily living behind, the mind is left with nothing to do. "What do you *think* about?" people ask me when they hear I spend hours on the road. They might be disappointed to hear that much of an ultra-runner's time is preoccupied with more or less the same concerns that occupy society in general: the problems of energy, food and water, shelter, health, self-defense, and waste. The difference is that whereas the runner in his place of work is responsible for only a minuscule *part* of a *section* of a *division* of one of life's innumerable problems, on the trail he takes responsibility for the entire universe of human survival, in microcosm. The runner in his office may be an Assistant Manager of bottle capping machine maintenance for a Southwestern North Carolina regional bottling plant. On the trail he is King of the World—the top decision maker, the nerve center coordinator in charge of all aspects of all things: the delivery of water and fuel to the cells; production and conservation of energy; regulation of heating and cooling; disposal of waste; and protection from external and internal threats. In short, the cerebral cortex of an ultra-runner, or at least the left side of it, is a very busy center of autonomous government, with no time for boredom or vacuous thumb-twiddling.

All this I was prepared for; it was only an extension of what I'd already learned in years of marathons and shorter races. Running Western States would be like sitting in the war room directing the logistics of a military campaign. Keep hydrated to within 3 percent of starting weight. Load on 10,000 calories between the start and mile 80. Reflect direct sunlight from the head in open areas, while optimizing evaporative and convective cooling in the shade, and so on and on. What I didn't fully realize was that this would also be a test of confronted by threats more insidious than exhaustion and dehydration.

As a high school English teacher some years ago, I had my students read William Golding's *Lord of Flies*, a disturbing vision of what can happen to the thin veneer of civilized behavior when people are put into a situation where survival is paramount. At Western States, I wasn't thinking of this as I approached the first aid station at Hodgson's Cabin about two hours into the race—the first chance to get water since the start. There was a well at the cabin from which a woman was busily drawing water and refilling the runners' bottles. I arrived about the same moment as two or three other runners, and hurriedly unscrewed the bottle lids to facilitate refilling. My hands raced to thrust my bottles forward first, before the other two or three, while my vision became a narrow tunnel aimed solely at the bottles. I did not see the faces of the other runners, only their waiting hands. Later, I would feel an odd remorse that I didn't offer to let the others refill first. I would understand too late that a better runner would have been not only better trained in the art of patience, but more understanding of the fact that a man's attitudes toward his fellows is closely connected to his attitudes toward the mountains, earth and sun; and his attitudes toward these things have, I suspect, profound impact on his ability to tap into the energy they contain.

The Western States 100 Mile Endurance Run has been called the world's ultimate test of endurance. When I first obtained a description of the course, it appeared that the most challenging features would be the huge quantity of climbing and descending; the high altitude; and the prevailing extremes of air temperature. As an Easterner, I found it hard to comprehend what I was reading. I found myself grasping for comparisons.

The climb in elevation from Katmandu, Nepal to the peak of Mt. Everest is 24,700 feet. In the Western States Run, there would be a total vertical ascent of 19,000 feet. There would also be a total *descent* of 21,000 feet—four vertical miles.

Then there was the altitude. A few weeks before Western States, race directors Norm and Helen Klein sent the runners a letter saying "the enclosed picture will give you an idea of what the first 4½ miles of the course look like." Enclosed was a glossy brochure of the Squaw Valley ski slopes, where the winter Olympics were held in 1960. A purple line marked the 2500-foot drop from Emigrant's Pass at 8700 feet to the valley floor 4½ miles below. The race would start at the bottom of the mountain and climb up the ski slope, which would still be capped with snow in late June. Trying to envision this, I recalled the time I ran the Mt. Washington Road Race in New Hampshire. That had been a June day too, a balmy 70 degrees at the foot of the mountain. The race climbed some eight miles to a rocky pinnacle that seemed to overlook the whole earth. The temperature was 35 and the wind lashed the naked peak at 60 mph. The elevation at the top of Mt. Washington was 6,288 feet—the highest place I had ever been. The *bottom* of the mountain at Squaw Valley, from which we would *begin* our climb in the Western States Run, was 6,200 feet.

Finally, there would be the challenge of heat. How do you dress for a race where you start out running on a snow-covered, wind-whipped mountain, then move on to four or five hours in 80-90 degree heat before reaching the first aid station where a crew member can take cast-off clothing? To start out with disposable clothing and discard it along the way—as is common in events like the Boston Marathon—would be out of the question. The Western States run follows an historic gold rush trail through some of the most beautiful wilderness in North America. Runners in this race are bound by a code that prohibits the slightest trace of their passage on the trail; so strictly is this code observed that even the toilet paper we carried had to be biodegradable. At a trail briefing the day before the race, we were gently warned that anyone who dropped so much as a fruit peel or paper cup on the trail would be immediately expelled.

I thought of all the road races I've run, where the runners have left a snowfall of paper cups on the pavement in their wake. I've always thought of distance runners as being more ecologically sensitive than most people; our activity brings us into closer daily contact with our physical environment, and perhaps gives us a greater appreciation of its nature. But runners are also deeply indoctrinated on the fragility of their own bodies, and especially on the need to drink sufficient water. We've all been told how a runner who flirts with dehydration flirts with spiraling temperature and death. In warm weather road races, this preoccupation with heat and dehydration takes precedence over any scruples about litter.

At Western States, the emphasis on water is even stronger—but with a radical difference. Runners are not merely cautioned about the difficulties of keeping hydrated in remote Sierra Nevada country; they are warned that if they become excessively dehydrated during the race they will be disqualified. We were informed that medical checks would be given at different points. Every runner would be weighed before the start and at each of these points. Anyone whose weight had dropped by seven percent or more at any of these checkpoints would be out of the race. Though most checkpoints are reachable only by four-wheel drive vehicles or horses, there would be 50 medical doctors and 75 nurses on the course. Yet, for all this emphasis, it was made abundantly clear that there would be no compromising of the larger life of the natural world— no littering or caches of personal supplies—to accommodate the needs of individual runners. Whatever we needed we must carry ourselves, whether in a fanny pack or in our hands; and whatever we carried into the forest we were expected to carry out. The usual order of ascendancy in the world was reversed here. The stars of this race would be the mountains, the vast wildflowered meadows of the Granite Chief Wilderness, the huge fir trees of Duncan Canyon, the cold fast water of the American River. We runners would be merely their visitors.

The dawn wind in the High Sierra is not just a passage of cool air through forest confers, but within the labyrinth of human con-

sciousness becomes a stirring of some world-magic of most delicate persuasion.—Ansel Adams

We started out a 5:00 a.m., running straight toward the moon. The first few seconds were surrealistic, as an ABC TV helicopter droned overhead and a huge bank of strobe lights lit us up for the cameras. Then we were out into the pre-dawn darkness and the business of settling into a comfortable pace.

Time began to telescope. The ascent to Emigrant's Pass was so easy as to be almost dreamlike. The sun broke across the mountain as we were crossing the snowfield approaching the peak, bathing the single file of runners' backs ahead of me with a golden light. There had been no gradual transition from night to morning; the light had washed across the mountain like a wave. The only other time I had ever seen a sunrise so sudden was during a plane flight across the Atlantic. I was sleepily gazing out of the window—as were, apparently, most of the people on my side of the plane—when the sun popped up out of the dark horizon bringing a spontaneous round of applause from the passengers. When the sun struck the snowfield on Emigrant's Pass, there was no applause; the runners were not spectators to the event but a part of it. I concentrated on efficiency, resisting any urge to rush. Shortly after passing the top, my watch beeped to signify that an hour had passed. We crossed into the Granite Chief Wilderness, gradually descending through fields of purple flowers. At Hodgson's Cabin the watch beeped again; and as the day progressed and we passed from cool morning to hot midday and afternoon, the beeping of the hours became itself a kind of rhythm.

The art of patience may be one of the most difficult lessons for an ultradistance runner to learn, particularly an American living in a world of fast-track lifestyles and rapidly diminishing attention spans. It is perhaps even more difficult for someone whose personal circumstances, as well as his culture, impose a sense of urgency. At the trail briefing the day before the race, I looked around at the runners. They looked like a typical group of rugged outdoors people, the kind of people you'd see backpacking or bicycling on a Saturday afternoon anywhere in America. They were lean, tanned, weathered. And they looked relaxed, good-natured, thoughtful. Most of them, men and women, had squint marks around their eyes. I couldn't help wondering if underneath those jocular T-shirts they were as casual and laid-back as they looked. I do not think people run 100 miles across the Sierra Nevada on impulse, the way they might adventurously go out for dinner at a Thai restaurant, or sign up for a weekend rafting trip in West Virginia. I did not inquire into the motives of these runners, but would guess that many, if not most of them, had very much more at stake than their casual demeanors would have suggested.

My old friend Jim Hall would probably tell me that if I live a life of insanely high stress, it's my own choice. But that doesn't necessarily mean I'm glad of that choice. Sometimes when you're driving in the fast lane, you get on to a road you can't get off.

Ten years ago, in a moment of impulsive romanticism, I started *Running Times* magazine. My initial capital was $75. The first issue was put together in a spare bedroom of my Washington, DC, townhouse. The accounting system was a paper bag. When subscription money came in I put it in the bag; when I needed money for supplies, I took it out of the bag. A friend who published a small newsletter had a little typesetting machine he said I could use when he wasn't in his office. He was in his office late every evening, so I got to do my production work mostly between midnight and dawn. His office was in a rundown building on Thomas Circle, the heart of Washington's prostitution district. My partners Phil Stewart and Rick Platt and I would work all day on editorial tasks at my house in Adams Morgan, then drive down to Thomas Circle for the type-setting and layout. We could never get in or out of our car without having to fend off the not very-subtle suggestions of half a dozen garishly painted Ladies of the Night. None of us knew anything about publishing; none of us had any business experience. We learned everything the hard way. The first six months, we typed all the mailing labels ourselves, sorted the magazine by zip code on my living room floor, and hauled them to the post office in my land Cruiser. We worked punishing hours, sometimes 36 hours straight. But we were young, full of enthusiasm, and driven by a dream. We were the most incompetent publishers in America, but we were in love with running and somehow that fact kept our magazine alive.

For the first couple of years were a wave of idealistic optimism. The work was exhausting, but I felt sustained by a vision of revo-lutionary change. Someday people were going to stop driving three miles to work, and would run or ride bikes. We'd stop being a na-tion of softies; we'd learn that physical and mental fitness go hand in hand. Going out to run was going to become as important to Americans as going out to eat. My own energy at the time seemed limitless. I played editor, publisher, writer, circulation manager, pro-duction manager, secretary, and errand boy—and was doing the best running of my life. In November, 1977 I ran the JFK 50 Mile—at that the time the country's largest ultramarathon with about 450 runners—and finished first. I was 36 years old and felt my life was just beginning. I had no way of knowing that the Age of Aquarius was already in its waning days.

It was around the third year that the trouble began. Until now we had printed a nice, honest magazine in brown ink on rough cream-colored paper. I thought this was an appropriate statement of the down-to-earth, no-nonsense values we represented. But the production cost per copy was too high, and I began to think of going on the newsstand to achieve better economies of scale. Some-one—I no longer recall who—told me that the newsstand whole-salers in the U.S. are organized along the same lines as certain other "family" run enterprises that permit no infringement on their ter-ritories. I was dubious, and tried to find a magazine consultant who could tell me what I was getting into. Oddly, none of the experts I called was able to help. They could advise me on direct mail, on ad-vertising, on editorial techniques, on any of a hundred aspects of the magazine trade—but not on newsstand distribution. To this day, I do not know what to believe. But I did go ahead and contact a national distributor, Publisher's Distributing Corporation, which urged me to start out with 100,000 newsstand copies. I agreed and went to PDC's plush New York offices to sign the contract. An ef-fusive executive arranged an advance on sales for our first nation-ally distributed issue, handed me a complimentary silver pen, and shook my hand. A few months later, the executive phoned to in-form me that sales of the first couple of issues had been a little dis-appointing, and we now owed the distributor something like

$40,000.

From that day, there began a slow leak of adrenaline into my bloodstream that has never ended. In November of that year I went back to the JFK 50 to defend my title. Midway through, I noticed a slight gurgling sound in my breathing and a weakness that hadn't bothered me the year before. I finished far behind the winner, exhausted. A doctor told me I had a case of walking pneumonia.

It wasn't until years later that my partners and I realized the irony of our situation: the more professional and sophisticated our magazine became, the more treacherous and demanding became the business challenges it presented—and the less prepared we were to meet them. The better the magazine looked, the richer people assumed we were, and the more targeted we became. I hired a man to help professionalize our operation and he promptly embezzled us, opening his own *Running Times* account in a Maryland bank. When presented with proof of fraud, the bank officials stiffly refused to cooperate, saying they were obligated to protect their depositor. A photographer we hired figured out that he could make more money doing extortion. With our limited funds hemorrhaging into the hands of thieves, we fought for survival by cutting staff and increasing our own workloads still further. This had two distressing effect: in order to meet our publishing deadlines we fell far behind in everything else, causing widespread irritations among everyone from contractors and correspondents to our own families; and we began to make increasing numbers of mistakes, One month we neglected to print the distributor's code on the cover, and had to reprint the cover at disastrous expense. Mistakes increased the pressure, which in turn produced more mistakes.

We all knew we were losing equilibrium when our running began to deteriorate. The loss of sleep, the financial struggle, and the general stress of impossible workloads began to take their toll. Rick, who had run a 2:23 marathon in the early years, was reduced to hobbling 12-minute miles. Phil, who had qualified for the Olympic Marathon trials in 1976, suffered a debilitating injury from which he has never fully recovered. I found myself trudging 15 to 20 miles per week and feeling chronically weary.

In 1981, with the birth of our first child, Sharon was suddenly afflicted with a severe illness. During the following two years she was to spend over 200 days in four different hospitals. At one point she was taken to a hospital in a severely dehydrated condition, then due to some blunder I shall never understand, was given no fluids for five more days and nearly died. My subsequent attempts to take legal action were stymied when I could find no doctor willing to testify against his colleagues at the negligent hospital. "I have to do business with those folks," said one physician. I was reminded of the uncooperative officials at the bank where our embezzled funds had been stashed, and began wondering how my expectations for the world had been so far off base. I felt disillusioned and defeated.

All of my non-working time was now needed for the care of my baby daughter Elizabeth, and for visiting Sharon in the hospital, and my running came to a halt. I've heard it said that runners who are forced by injuries or illness to stop running become monsters. That didn't happen to me; I didn't scream and rant in the office. I became a walking vortex of deadly silence. I received little sympathy from staff or family, all of whom walked in wide circles around me as though I were a coil of electrified barbed wire.

As I was eventually to discover in a place called Deadwood Canyon, there is always a low point. At work, my brain wouldn't turn over in the morning without a 16 oz. shot of coffee. By 4 p.m., I would feel as though any minute I might collapse—simply topple over on the floor. I hadn't been to a doctor in seven years, and recalling the righteous chiding I'd given my soon-to-be-late friend Jim Fixx, I went for a physical. I passed the stress test without difficulty, getting the maximum possible score on the Bruce protocol. But a blood test revealed that I had a hypothyroid condition. My doctor, who is a runner himself, was vague about what this meant or what had caused it, but assured me that I'd be able to live a perfectly normal life as long as I took thyroid supplement for the rest of my days. While he was out of the room, I looked up hypothyroidism in one of his medical books. The principal symptoms are "cretinism" and "gross obesity." That, I thought, is a fine kettle of fish for a distance runner trying to make a living as an editor!

If this were the movies, that would have been a clear turning point. I would have gone out for a punishing 10-miler that very night, and sent in my entry to the world's toughest footrace the very next morning. But in real life, things are rarely so neat. My memory—perhaps diminished by creeping hypothyroidism—is not clear on just when the turning point actually occurred. Maybe it was the day I discovered we had just made a $6,000 printing mistake. A running shoe company had asked us to reprint their two-page ad from an earlier issue, and somehow we had picked up the left-hand page from one ad with the right-hand page from another. We had no choice but to reprint the entire 16-page section in which the ad appeared—a 10-second proofreading error having wiped out our meager profit for the year. Or maybe the turning point was when we found we'd been defrauded by a large mail order runner's shop. The company placed a 16-page advertising insert, then immediately after the magazine had been printed and shipped, informed us they had just filed for bankruptcy. We saw them several times after that doing a booming business at various road race expos, raking in the cash but never paying us a penny.

Ultimately, I think it was none of these specific body punches that brought me to a crisis decision, but the spreading cynicism I felt toward the whole running business. Throughout the 30 years I had been a runner, the thing that had always most energized me was the simple *joy* of running. The thing that had given me my biggest kicks in *Running Times* was publishing photos of men, women, and children experiencing that joy-leaping spontaneously at the finish line, hugging, laughing and crying with the emotion of achievement. It appalled me that I should be spending my time stalking around my office seething with anger and frustration over bad business deals, and dreading to take phone calls from the very community I had once most loved. It saddened me that I could have become such a negative person writing about such a positive subject. Above all, it frightened me that I should have become such a zombie—such a dark-spirited and listless man—posing as an authority on one of life's most energizing activities.

Looking back over the past 10 years, I realized that what had occurred was a gradual loss of psychic reserves. When I started the magazine I was sitting on a bank account of tremendous endurance built up over 20 years of running combined with a relatively secure professional and family life. In those first hard years of my magazine, I handled my workload enthusiastically because of those accumulated reserves. But the continuing struggles of my job, along with the added stress of Sharon's illness, had used those reserves up. My doctor was optimistic, but I knew where I was headed. The hypothyroidism was merely the weakest link—the first to go. If I did not restore the reserves soon, I would indeed join my friend Jim Fixx in that place where runners never need to train.

A rational decision would have been to restore strength through progressive increases in training and racing distance; this is the advice I give to anyone recovering from a long layoff. But the urgency of my condition somehow precluded rationality. Ever since that magical autumn of 1956 when I first joined my high school cross-country team as a 15-year-old, my whole sense of identity had been tied to my running. To lose my running after three decades was to lose my life, and all memory of my life. Emotionally, if not physically, I was desperate; like a gambler at the bottom of his luck, I was ready to bet everything on a single toss of the dice.

The Western States Endurance Run came to me like a prophet's vision. There could be no salvation in working my way slowly back to life through half-hearted 5Ks and 10Ks. Too vivid were the memories of how good—how *alive*—I had felt in training for the JFK a decade ago, and how adventurous the challenges of the magazine had been in the early years when I was a young Bob Feller and my fast ball could never fail. Maybe the fact that I was now 44 years old added to the urgency. The last thing in the world I wanted was moderation or compromise. The Western States 100 was the toughest major footrace in the world. To finish it was the most uncompromising test of endurance there was, and I needed to pass that test. Eight months before the race, I sent for an entry form and the next morning I got up at 5:30 a.m. and laced on my most durable pair of training shoes.

During the first hours of the race, the vision crystallized to a hard clear reality. Loping down the rocky trail from Red Star Ridge to Duncan Canyon at 24 miles, I felt light and free, like a butterfly released from its cocoon. I had trained well for the distance, doing at least 30 runs of 30 miles or longer in the preceding eight months. A short distance beyond Duncan Canyon, I commented to another runner, "Well, we've just done a marathon." He responded with the economical chuckle of a man who feels good now but has 74 miles to go. I felt fine, except for a noticeable tiredness in my quadriceps. After our 2500-foot climb to Emigrant's Pass we had done over two hours of downhill running, some of it quite steep, and I wasn't used to putting on the brakes so much.

My biggest concern was with keeping adequately hydrated and fueled. The logistics of food and water supply are unusually difficult at Western States because of the inaccessibility of the terrain. There are just three aid stations—accessible only by jeep and horse—before the Robinson Flat checkpoint at 30 miles. At the trail briefing the day before, I had learned that this 30-mile point would be the first point where support crews could reach the course by car. Roads were so roundabout that it would take 3½ hours of driving from the starting line to get there. Sharon was to meet me there with food and glucose drink. Bob Cooper, our Western Editor, would meet me at the Deep Canyon II checkpoint at 36 miles. After that, it would be Sharon again at Michigan Bluff (56 miles). Michigan Bluff would be a significant landmark, because once you've reached that point all the toughest parts of the course are behind you.

With only three water stops in our first 29 miles, everyone had to carry water. Most runners wore water belts. I had tried one for the first time about 10 days before the start, wearing it with two full 16-ounce bottles of water for a 2½ hour run. It was comfortable enough, but the next day there was an ominous ache in my lower back. I decided to go with a pair of Hanteens instead. These are plastic bottles shaped like Heavy Hands; they are easy to hold and contain 12 fluid ounces in each hand. The 24 ounces wouldn't be as much as the 32 carried by two belt bottles, but with all the downhill running I faced I thought it would be foolish to add further stress to my back. My only regret was that I'd have to go so far before replenishing supplies. I had planned to keep myself hydrated with a glucose polymer drink—the most effective means of replenishing carbohydrate—throughout the race. I figured to consume the initial 24 ounces in the first 10 miles, and with no crew access until Robinson Flat I'd then have to go a 20-mile stretch in the morning sun with no glucose replacement. In that stretch I'd at least eat a few cookies from a drop bag at 17 miles, and drink as much water as possible.

We'd been warned about the heat. It seemed surprising to me that there could be any place in North America where you could go through snow and a 100-degree sun in the same run. But that has been the prevailing pattern at Western States. Official temperatures reached 98 in 1983, 101 in '84. In the canyons, we were warned it would be much hotter—generally around 110.

My worst nightmare was that I'd be medically disqualified due to dehydration. My body is not shy about sweating. I have excellent heat tolerance, but in 90-plus temperatures I can easily lose 10 pounds in a three hour run. At a starting weight of 144 pounds, with a seven percent limit, an 11-pound loss at any point in a run that could go 24 hours or longer would put me out of the game. In the pre-race briefing, one of the race officials had noted that runners often take an "adversarial" attitude toward the doctors. She urged us to understand that the doctors were really out there to help us, not impede us, and would "work with us" to get us through. Indeed, I was conscious of their support at each of the aid stations. At the 24-mile checkpoint, a doc cheerfully exhorted us to "tank up now, so you'll be ready for that first major medical in six miles!" By now we were into the heat of the day, and while I was re-filling my Hanteens and drinking at every opportunity, I was nervous about the weight check as I came into Robinson Flat and was hustled onto the scale (weigh first, drink later). I had never run a marathon without becoming extremely dehydrated. Amazingly, my weight at 30 miles was exactly the same as my starting weight. Exhilarated, I tanked up on Sharon's cookies, a cup of fresh fruit, coffee, and more glucose polymer, and set out on the trail for Deep Canyon II.

At 40 miles, Bob Cooper met me with a peanut butter and jelly sandwich, more cookies, and more glucose. I noticed that I was beginning to dislike eating. Reminding myself that I'd need an estimated 15,000 calories in the course of the run, and had probably stored only about a third of that in the form of muscle glycogen, I choked down half the sandwich. I was unable to touch the cookies, which looked about as appetizing to me as cowpies. I moved on impatiently, perhaps too impatiently.

At 43 miles we reached the ghost town called Last Chance. According to a local historian, "This mining town was probably named for the prospector who used his last bullet to shoot a deer after the miners ran out of food. On the other hand, it could have been named after one miner said to another, 'Now this is the last chance. If there's no gold in this pan, we leave.'" I have a simpler explanation: this is, simply, the last chance to turn back before descending into Deadwood Canyon.

From the stories I had heard about the 110-degree temperatures in the canyons, I had envisioned deep chasms of sunblasted rock, like narrow cousins of the Grand Canyon. Much to my surprise, I found Deadwood to be heavily forested, and the temperature probably no higher than 90. But the trail descended steeply in a series of precipitous switchbacks, and in less than 10 minutes I had gone beyond any downhill in my experience. After 20 minutes, I became acutely conscious of my toes; they were smashing into the fronts of my shoes, and I was beginning to stub them with painful regularity. My quadriceps, unaccustomed to such continuous braking, were beginning to ache. I moved slower and slower, feeling as though I was running barefoot on shards of glass. It took me an hour to reach the bottom, at which point the trail crossed a small footbridge over a stream, and started back up. As I began the ascent, I felt suddenly overwhelmed. I was dizzy—whether from heat or loss of altitude I can't say—and my quads were shot. As I struggled upward, I talked with another runner who had stopped briefly to sit on a rock. "The next canyon is just as bad," he said. At the top of the canyon, a place called Devil's Thumb, there was a medical check. I had lost four pounds in four miles.

The truth is that I don't remember the next canyon, Eldorado, quite as clearly. Whatever it was that happened to me happened in Deadwood Canyon. The rest of the way down to Eldorado and back up to Michigan Bluff, I was mostly preoccupied with what I would say to Sharon and Elizabeth, to all the people I had told I was going to run this race (putting everything on this one throw of the dice), if I decided to quit.

It's amazing how much difference in attitude a little sugar in the brain can make, as I discovered a few hours later—a few hours too late. In retrospect, coming into Michigan Bluff might have been a cause for celebration, or at least for reviving hope. It was just after six p.m.; I had been running for 13 hours and had gotten through the toughest parts of the course. I was still on schedule for a 24-hour finish, and that had been my goal: to win the coveted silver belt buckle awarded to all who finish in 24 hours or less. I was still three hours ahead of the cutoff pace. My quads were dead, but I wouldn't be needing them for several hours. But that's the perspective that came later.

What I did at the time was to walk over to an official and say, "I'm dropping out." I held out my right arm, the one with the medical wristband which must be surrendered if you leave the race. Remembering this, I flash back to the time I watched a dramatic ninth inning home run win a world series game—I don't recall the year. What I remember is the comment of the pitcher who threw the home run ball: "As soon as I let go of the ball, I thought *oh no . . .*" As the official clipped off my band with her scissors, I knew how that pitcher felt.

Epilogue

Runners can get through the weary and lonely hours only if they are . . . at peace with themselves. —Antonio Rossman, a San Francisco attorney who finished in 28:45:25.

To trivialize a significant experience is to lose sight—however momentarily—of the larger picture. I think of my five-year-old, Elizabeth, who became so upset with a small scratch on her knee during a visit to her playground that her whole visit was ruined. On a sunny afternoon in the High Sierras of California, I became so distressed about the condition of the downhill-running muscles of my upper legs that I lost touch with the fundamental soundness of the rest of my body. I also lost touch with my primary objective: to finish the race. Though days have passed, I still wake up in a sweat wondering what might have happened if I had eaten and rested for half an hour, then *walked* out of Michigan Bluff in no hurry, content to wait until I felt ready to break into a jog.

My ultimate error was one of impatience. It's ironic, because patience is what I had coached myself in most. The night before the start, I wrote myself a note: *"Run with the sun, not with the shooting stars."* Indeed, throughout my long day in the Sierra Nevada, I successfully avoided all entanglements of competition. I moved easily, conserved energy successfully, and felt time pass like a mountain breeze. But in the shock of contemplating my exhausted quads at Michigan Bluff, I became impatient to resolve the agony. I thought of this a few days after the race, when I went for a run with Ken Lee in San Francisco; as we crossed over the Golden Gate Bridge, Ken told me about the hundreds of people who have jumped off. "Some of them just leave their car doors open and their motor running, and take a run," he said.

I heard a happier story a few days later. I was talking with Tom O'Neil of Butte, Montana, who ran most of the way with a wrenched left knee. O'Neil, who finished in 29:10:54, said that at one point—he couldn't remember where—he was sitting in a medical tent next to a young man named Bill McKean, who had taken a bad fall and dislocated his shoulder. The shoulder was heavily bandaged, and McKean felt hopelessly immobilized. "He said there was no way he could continue, and he was going to cut off his wristband," remembered O'Neil. "He was about to do it, and I said, 'No, don't! Just wait awhile and think it over. You have plenty of time.' He waited, and later I saw him at the finish. He got through."

For me, I suppose the most blatant error of impatience was the belief that I could make up nine years of falling behind in one grand run; that I could cleanse the bad blood of all my anxieties with one day of clean High Sierra air. It took a billion years for those mountain to be built and those canyons to be carved. If I'm to learn the patience necessary to deal with them on their terms, I'll have to start by training for those hellacious downhills—and waiting—for twelve more months.

THE 37-MILE UNMARKED INVISIBLE ACID TEST

Tom Hart

A sunny day in early December, I could see Boston's glossy skyscrapers, the Prudential Center and the John Hancock Building, in the distance as I trotted through the considerably less shiny neighborhoods of Somerville across the river. It was about noon of a wonderfully unseasonable early winter running day, temperatures climbing through the 40s, and I mentally checked off details as I ran.

Let's see . . . I'd just made a stop to change into fresh running clothes, and my daypack held another dry jersey and a T-shirt if I needed them. Had I remembered to bring those socks I wanted to exchange in Harvard Square? Yep. I had some money in the pocket of my all-weather running suit. Legs felt pretty loose. My stomach —those just-gulped cookies and that quick swig of milk sloshing around in it—seemed okay. The 14-plus mile suburban loop out to Lexington and back was behind me now. Only a little over 22 to go, and still reasonably close to schedule. My 37-mile run on my 37th birthday was progressing satisfactorily. The only detail that remained slightly fuzzy as I set out, the only question to which I couldn't fire back a fast answer, was surely the most interesting one. Why was I doing this?

"It seemed like a good idea at the time," would have been as valid an answer as any, I suppose. I'd considered the run more carefully than that, however, and had reasons enough, or at least enough to satisfy me. In the first place, 37 miles on my 37th birthday was a project that had that kind of quirky numerical logic to which a great many runners, myself included, are addicted. A large part of running's charm, after all, is that it generates such a wealth of precise numbers, numbers we can squirrel away in our logs as fastests, farthests, and other personal treasures.

Also, I was strongly drawn to the novelty of the experience. I'd never run farther than the marathon distance, which meant that this journey would take me through more than 10 miles of unexplored territory. I can't believe there are many runners who haven't wondered what would happen if they got out there five, 10 or more miles beyond their previous longest run. I hadn't extended my horizons so precipitously since my first marathon, over five years earlier.

Finally, beyond this desire to make a cautious dip into the ultra-running waters, I had decided that a run was the perfect birthday present to myself. And a fine extravagant one it was, too: a gift of the day, set aside for only this run of ridiculous and glorious length.

໖

So I had plenty of perfectly good reasons to be out there ambling all over town, or towns, more properly: Somerville, Arlington, Lexington, Cambridge, Boston. I started out at about a 7:45 or so pace, more than half a minute per mile slower than I usually train, and every three or four miles I'd walk for about five minutes. The plan was to take it easy throughout, and to be finished after roughly six hours (though I confess I harbored the secret hope that I could do it in closer to five.)

I was in decent shape for such an expedition. A month earlier I'd run my fastest marathon in a little under 2:45. Aside from a low-key five-mile race two weeks after that, I'd not done any hard running work since, but I'd kept plugging along at 55 to 60 miles a week. I felt quite confident (innocent that I was!) about going the full distance, even though I couldn't really imagine what those last five or 10 miles would feel like.

For the morning loop, the first stage of the run, I'd headed out to Lexington, a familiar route. About halfway there I'd walked for a bit, and then had walked again when I got to the center of Lexington itself. Buying a giant cookie and some juice (I'd not wanted to have to carry anything heavier than money on this first stage) stretched this break to nearly 10 minutes as I strolled around Battle Green and the Minuteman statue.

Heading homeward out of town I'd passed an old-fashioned iron direction post on a little circle at a place where the road split. Reading its mileages—CONCORD 7, STONEHAM 8, LOWELL 16, BOSTON 12—and knowing I was going to run farther than any of these had given me a fine feeling of freedom. After another short walk about halfway back, I'd arrived back at my house in Somerville feeling pretty fresh. A short change-and-eat break and then I shoved off again, doing my mental checklist.

I felt good—and yet below the surface somewhere, a rankling feeling of unfulfilled expectation. Aside from that brief flash at the signpost, these two-plus hours hadn't quite achieved the specialness I'd hoped for. The epic quality of the run hadn't made itself felt and I was impatient, looking for something, well . . . new.

My first break on this second stage of the run came just two miles later. It turned out to last slightly longer than expected, as exchanging my splendid but overlarge birthday gift socks became moderately complex. Just entering the store was a come-down: It seemed tiny and dark after a morning spent in the sunny expanses of my journey. Then there was the clerk, a tall, weedy fellow engaged, when I arrived, in what seemed to me particularly trivial chatter with some lingering customers. Dealing with people after two and a half hours on the road, in the middle of a long run, is not unlike dealing with people right after you've become a parent. You're extremely alert, even speedy. You expect everyone to recognize instinctively a special quality about you and to treat you with tremendous consideration. Anything less grates; you get grumpy. Doesn't this fellow know I have 20 miles still to run? Can't he devote a little attention to someone engaged in so noble a project?

When the clerk did, finally, turn to me, prompt answers to my questions seemed beyond him. I mean, come on! How hard could it be for him to come up with a smaller pair of those snappy brown argyles for a terrific guy like me, a hero of the road? Leaving, I grumped my way over to the river and down to MIT, where I met my one pre-arranged mid-run connection of the day. I'd told my friend Stephen that I'd be there around 12:30, figuring that gave me ample margin for error, but my schedule, loose though it was, was already breaking down, and I got there closer to one o'clock. The last five miles, with breaks, had taken about 50 minutes. Stephen handed me some apple juice, and after walking with him for a few minutes I pushed off again. Over the bridge to the Boston side and back upriver.

I wasn't exactly tired at that point, but a growing realization began to take hold. I'd been on this run for three and a half hours and had hours still to go. The sheer amount of time on my feet was going to become a critical factor. I remembered Bill Rodgers' remark about the toughness of four-hour marathoners, how he respected their ability to keep on their feet and hard at it for so long, something he never has to do. Although I hadn't gone into a new distance range yet, I was on the edge of running for a longer time than ever before. And with well over two hours still ahead, I was getting my first glimpse of the size of the task I'd taken on. I began to see that one element in the new equation I was creating as I ran was a certain undercurrent, not altogether undesirable, of fear.

I really needed the water-and-stretching stop at the Harvard boat-house after crossing the river again at about 23 miles, and was glad to take another break a few miles later as I neared Fresh Pond Reservoir in Cambridge. Here I made a side trip to a little store where I picked up my last provisions. I ate as I walked, and finished the carob-raisin-nut snack and apple juice as I arrived at the pond.

I had by now almost covered the marathon distance, about four and a quarter hours after starting out. I was entering what I'd envisioned as the third and last stage of my trip. I was very tired now, but here I would find my reward, here each mile would surely be special. Five laps of the two-and-a-quarter-mile main course around the reservoir, with a walk to begin each lap, would take me to the magic 37 mark.

ﻹ

Runners generally have some route on which they feel most comfortable, some course they consider their running "home." Fresh Pond was certainly mine, and arriving there gave this fading novice ultra-runner a much-needed psychological lift. Here I was also able to check my progress against mile markers, and was pleasantly surprised to find that I was still moving along—when running—at not too far above an eight-minute pace.

I was tight, I was slowing, but I was going to make it. Probably. I hadn't doubted that when I began, but back there nearly 30 miles and four and half hours ago the miles were abstract, and each new one now was assuming laborious reality.

I had read Tom Osler's excellent training books, and had also virtually memorized James Shapiro's wonderful reports from the ultra front. Osler made his point clearly: If one was in shape to run a 2:45 marathon, one could quite conceivably (with a careful approach) break seven hours in a 50-mile race. One could, given a decent running background, double one's longest run by mixing walking and running and by drinking lots of fluids, preferably sugary ones.

My 37-mile run had thus seemed imminently possible, even something of a lark, and I'd decided the key was to approach it with a light-hearted attitude, with no rigidly set goal for the time it would take. This enlightened view, sensible as it was, didn't help my legs feel better when they tightened up as 30 miles came and went and I passed the five-hour mark. I'd imagined myself occasionally stopping during the day to gaze at pleasant vistas along the river, thinking great thoughts while surges of well-being and accomplishment filled me. All who saw me would intuitively understand the magnitude of my achievement. Instead, here I was, struggling along in total anonymity, no doubt the most mundane-seeming of pedestrians. Never had I been so aware of the essential privacy of the running experience. Instead of runner's high, I was experiencing what might be called "the incognito effect."

Everything since leaving my apartment that morning had taken on a double hue. There was what I knew I was doing, and then there was what anyone observing me might have thought I was doing. The longer I ran, the wider the gulf between the two became. That much of life operates under this same principle was little comfort to aching tendons. Was it for this meager insight that I'd set aside the day? It was continuously, if mildly, irritating to see other runners, none of whom—naturally enough—stopped to inquire about or marvel at what I was doing. I mean, the wisdom of a few hours' distance had allowed me to see the foolishness of having expected any kind of understanding from that clothing store clerk, but surely these runners ought to pay more respectful attention? Instead, they were ignoring me. Worse, they were passing me! Damn, how galling! Losing flying speed, it was hard not to begin to be obsessed with finishing this thing. My vision narrowed, my thoughts shrank. No vistas, no glimpses of far-off buildings, no sociological speculation or psychological breakthroughs. My view closed down mile by mile. As I circled Fresh Pond, the beautiful reservoir was on my right constantly, woods or a golf course on my left; these became the blacktop stretching ahead, then just the path directly in front of me. The leather toe reinforcement between black rubber sole and blue nylon shoe upper revealed a fascinating texture to which I'd clearly never paid enough attention.

I began to imagine slowing, slowing, until finally I stopped, terminally absorbed in some minute pebble pattern in the path's surface invisible to anyone else. The appeal of such cessation grew dangerously.

I bumped into a friend on my third lap, and that helped. Ordinary running-talk, what he would do in his next race, what I'd done in my last one, served to distract me and we got through a mile or so not far off eight-minute pace before parting. That was the good news. The bad news was that the minimal extra effort it had taken just to stay with his graciously slowed pace, just about wiped me out. Margin for error dwindles, then disappears, beyond the marathon distance, and I'd overspent. My break-walk after that lap didn't help much. Nor did mental games, like trying to stay close behind a woman who jogged past me. She pulled away effortlessly. I struggled through, needing an unscheduled rest halfway through. The afternoon was slipping away now, cooling perceptibly as the sun's rays thinned. I was very tight, the lap absurdly long.

The final circuit, by contrast, was comparatively easy. Knowing it was almost over had restored some of the run's elusive magic.

Fears of not being able to finish disappeared as the end beckoned just two miles, then one, then less, away. The joy that began to make itself felt was suddenly somewhat tempered by regret that soon I'd be leaving this little world of the run to rejoin the real one. The world of others, of obligations. Still I was happy, slogging toward the finish at somewhere near a nine-minute pace. Happily beat. How wrong I'd been at the outset to consider my start a conservative one!

After six hours and 10 minutes, or almost exactly an average of 10 minutes per mile covered overall, I ground blissfully to a stop at the pond's upper parking lot. I wish I could report the thrilling details of the finishing celebration but, appropriately enough, there was no celebration. My wife was waiting with the car, and I simply clambered into the gray Toyota and we went home. Inside of half an hour I was soaking in a hot bath, enjoying a mighty feeling of satisfaction.

I had worried some about how my body would recover, but in fact wasn't beset by any special aches and pains in the next few days of running. I noticed a change in attitude, though. My psychological capital had been depleted, and the drive to get out and run was all but gone. A consecutive running streak of a year's length ended within 10 days, and my yearly mileage goals were revised downward as December diminished. It was somehow pleasingly consistent to me that the after-effects of the run proved to be no more what I'd expected than the run itself. After all, the point had been to pursue the unexpected.

Having that day for my own purposes, and making something satisfying of it was, to me at least, reward enough. And if the others might not see it the way I did . . . well, that was the lesson of the "incognito effect," wasn't it? It can't hurt to be reminded from time to time of the necessity of making one's own satisfactions, and of the futility of expecting anyone else to understand them. The gulf between what we feel we're doing and what others perceive us to be doing will remain the most ultra of all distances, one that no amount of miles, or words, can finally bridge.

RUNNING WILD ON THE TAMESIDE

Mark Will-Weber

"Bite on the bullet, old man, and don't let them think you're afraid." —Rudyard Kipling

D ay two I remember vividly. I was racing across the twisting trail atop Hobson Moor. The three-mile climb had reduced my oxygen intake to an uneven rasp, as if each breath needed to be hauled all the way up from the soles of my battered waffle racers. My quads simmered on slow burn.

Spectators clustered along the top of the moor, their cheers sounding fuzzy and far away. Abruptly, a British gent—slightly gray around the temples and wearing the traditional flatcap—leaned in and burred in my ear: "Come on, lad! Grind 'em out! Grind 'em out!"

I honed in on the runner just in front of me, then we plunged over the lip. Ahead of us, rolling down to the finish, lay two miles of stone-strewn slopes. I began negotiations with the Supreme Being: "Please, God, get me down. Get me down in one piece and—I promise—I'll never do anything stupid again."

But that was in another country. My stupidity had commenced back in the States, months before, where I enjoyed leafing through the racing brochure, reading each little synopsis of the individual stages that comprise the "Tour of Tameside." A course description that includes the word "undulating" looks great on the written page, and I liked the little maps, too.

The 1989 "Tour of Tameside," chiefly sponsored by Thomas Cook and promoted by Ron Hill Sports, was billed in the race brochure as the "toughest challenge in British athletics." That claim is not without foundation. The diabolical brainchild of famed British marathoner and streak Hill, the "Tour"—six races over a seven-day span—kicked off in 1981. Hill modeled his event after cycling's Tour de France, with races of various distances and terrains. The total tour adds up to a double marathon (52 miles), and final places are determined by accumulated time. The week before I left for England, I'd sit in my office cubicle, feigning any real work, and daydream about racing strategies for each course, each day, as if there were some fantastic trick to it, and all I really needed to do was figure out precisely what the trick was: Houdini before the Gates of Hell, ready to unveil the grand finale.

What I loved most, though, was the promise of impending adventure. There were no initial deals with God or the Devil. Just me, racing in England. Me, striding smoothly through quaint stone villages and the green countryside. Me, hoisting a few pints of ale in postrace camaraderie with the local lads at ye old town pub. That's what I envisioned.

Once in England, we (wife Sally at the rent-a-car wheel) drove northwest from London to Hyde, a working class town of factories and shops (not unlike Bethlehem, Pennsylvania, where I live and run) located on the edge of the urban sprawl known as Greater Manchester. Along the way, I got unexpected advice on the Tour. In Buxton, a village in the rugged Peak District of Derbyshire, I met Billy—a friendly bloke wearing a black T-shirt and purple-blue tattoos on each forearm—shooting pool at the local pub. A former runner ("When I weighed a few stone less, mind you") who looked more like a rugby player, Billy said he'd run the Tour back in1984. "I heard the Tour's pretty tough," I offered.

Billy winced, took a long pull on his pint of stout, then wiped the foam off his handlebar mustache. The British Open jabbered on the telly in the background, and another patron—an Andy Capp kind of chap—scratched the weathered ears of a black and white border collie that snoozed at his feet.

"Tough?" Billy roared. (To my untrained ear it sounded more like "Toouff?" "Why it's bloody hell (blood-E 'ell)!" He rapped home a shot, the length of the tattered table, for effect. When I left, Billy from Buxton wished me luck. Two hours later, I picked up my number at Ron Hill's Running Wild athletics shop in Hyde. My racing bib was No. 13. How lucky can you get?

Day 1: Sunday, July 23 11-Mile Run Across Tameside (Hyde to Mossley)

"I see you stand like greyhounds in the slips, straining upon the start." —William Shakespeare, *Henry VIII*

Everybody who stands on the starting line for a stage race has some kind of story, and this was mine: Journalist, lured by trip to England, running chiefly to observe, experience and write. My main goal? Finish. Secondary goal? Avoid serious injury and/or embarrassment.

It was a little unsettling, then, to meet the Ron Hill Sports people and other runners at The Village Hotel (our home base in Hyde, complete with—ahh, yes—a hot whirlpool bath!) who inevitably greeted me with: "Oh, so you must be the American . . ." Being "the American" sounded too much like I was one of the invited elites, expected to joust with the leaders day after day.

The "invited elites," included runners like Eddy Hellebuyck, the diminutive two-time champ ('84 and '87) from Belgium; Henning Soegaard, a promising young runner from Denmark; and Catherine Newman, a quiet lass from the Exeter Harriers, the top female entrant. Eleanor Adams, a world-class ultramarathon veteran, actually ran the Tour to "prep" for a string of world and British ultra records she'd set later that summer. Then there were, of course, the British runners—a slew of gritty club racers, mostly from working-class roots. The local lads—from places like Stockport, Manchester, Liverpool—weren't exactly weaned on cricket or grass-court tennis. The best of them were smaller, faster versions of Billy from Buxton. Tough guys. Most of them did a full day's work, ran a stage of the Tour, then got up and did it all again. In all, nearly 600 runners took on the Tameside Tour (so named because the River Tame runs through the region). On day one, we gathered at a big stone building, Hyde's town Hall, to "sign in" a la tour de France cyclists.

I signed my name next to No. 13 (my race number) on a big sheet of white cardboard. Five empty places to sign, each representing a race to be run, remained. A race volunteer at the table must have read my mind, and smiled: "Later in the week, when the runners get more and more tired, you can hardly read their writing."

And so it began. With Britain in the grip of a rare heat wave (high 80s) and a full Tour ahead, it seemed logical to start conservatively.

What I learned on day one was that logical people don't sign up for the Tour. The pack blasted off, right from the opening gun—Mad Dogs and Englishmen in the noonday sun, pounding past the fish 'n' chips shop and rows of gray stone houses with white lace curtains in the windows.

I hit two miles faster than I wished, about 10:20, and I estimated I was barely in the top 50. Either there were a helluva lot of faster runners up there, or a lot of guys were going to melt in the heat. As we rolled through residential areas, both assumptions proved true.

I latched onto a steady, fast-moving pack and—bingo—it hit

me. This was the way to run the whole Tour: Start out controlled, hook up with an aggressive but sane group that appeared to be moving up and simply feast on the foolishly ambitious—like sharks.

Our little pack included a pony-tailed "veteran" (40-plus—the English equivalent to a U.S. "master") named Rob Taylor, a tough, wily runner from nearby Stockport. He called up to me: "All the way, USA!" We shared some water, then worked together the rest of the run. Somewhere near the Heroes of Waterloo pub at the base of a two-mile long hill up to Mossley, we moved into the top 20. By the time we finished on the soccer field at the Mossley Football Club, I was 16th (1:37). Hellebuyck smashed the field with a record 55:26, already more than a minute up on second in the Tour overall standings. Even with five races left, he assumed the role of strong favorite and donned the fluorescent lime "leader's singlet."

After the race, I got a rubdown from the Tour masseur, Diego Maggio. You could tell the runners who'd done the Tour before because they always made a beeline for the massage table. Diego was used to kneading big-muscled pro cyclists, so rubbing down skinny little distance runners was simple. The guy had the hands of a major-league baseball catcher.

When I got off the table, I felt brand new. Joyful runners crammed in the Mossley clubhouse, and more than a few thirsty participants knocked back pints of stout and ale. Stage One was done, and celebration reigned. It was a lot like I dreamed it would be, and I felt, well, euphoric. I *could* race the Tour, and maybe crack the top ten.

Then I bumped into Ron Hill. He was both directing and running in the Tour. "Tomorrow's tougher," Hill promised. "The Hill Run. I'm picking my way down." He held up his hand as explanation. "Broke my wrist at the bottom one year." Not what I wanted to hear. On the Tour, too much knowledge can hold you back. Ignorance, on the other hand, now there was something that could get you to the finish line.

Day 2: Monday, July 24
6-Mile "Hill Run"
(Copley, Stalybridge)

Half a league, half a league Half a league onward Into the valley of Death Rode the six hundred Forward the Light Brigade! Was there a man dismayed?
—Alfred, Lord Tennyson, *The Charge of the Light Brigade*

Always the student of history, it was not lost on me that the number of runners in the Tour of Tameside closely approximated those in the British Cavalry's ill-fated "Charge of the Light Brigade" during the Crimean War. A French general who witnessed the blunderous attack from a far bluff pronounced in disbelief: "It is magnificent, but it is not war. . . ." The Tour of Tameside is a similar spectacle. How splendid we looked, lined up in our multicolored shorts and singlets, dashing madly between lines of spectators each day, toasting our exploits by night, and then waking to do it again. It could pump you up—and sweep you away, too.

But day two—the Six-Mile Hill Run—was a lot like charging the Russian cannons in the Crimea. The reasons why rapidly got hazy. You couldn't think about it too much, or you might come to your senses and neglect to sign in. For most of the Brits—experienced "fell runners"—this was an opportunity to kick butt.

We lined up on a bridge in the middle of a reservoir. With a 7:30 p.m. start, the heat was subsiding. The leaders blitzed into high gear, oblivious to what awaited. A first mile in 4:50 barely put me in the top 30; the front-runners were a good 20 seconds ahead. Then we turned left—actually, turned "up" would be more accurate. Legs that felt "good" after day one rapidly felt "raced in." One glance at the climbing, winding road, one listen to the wheezing pack, and you knew it would only get worse. I forced myself to pass runners all the way to the top of Hobson Moor, knowing full well I'd need a cushion on the way down.

At the top I ran in a dream state through an expanse of rock and thistle that was Hobson Moor. Up came ol' "Grind 'em out," urging in my ear. The way he said "Gr" made me think of a garbage truck changing rusty gears. You could no more ignore him than you could ignore pain itself, though certainly he meant well. Still, his exhortations irritated me. "Grind 'em out!" What the hell did that mean? Grind out the miles? Grind out the competition?

Fatigue and anger make a poor parachute. We whipped around a small marker at the top, then plunged over the edge of the fell. Suddenly, all anger was gone, swept out the back door, and there was only fatigue, quads as useless as burned-out brakes and a shooting, electric current of fear. *Real* fear. Fear of falling, fear that the runner behind or ahead of me might fall, fear of shattered limbs or skulls. My concerns were reflected on the faces of race volunteers, posted on the mountainside, hands held high and ready to pluck out any would-be Humpty Dumpties. Experienced British fell runners, including Rob Taylor, zipped by on my right and left. Still, I also passed people, not by design but merely by bounding through the air, triple-jump style, and miraculously landing on tufts of grass and even, on occasion, the slithering snake of a trail. About halfway down, I caught the tip of my waffle on a large rock but somehow stayed upright. Later, I heard one runner blew out his shoe—ripped on the rocks—then begged a new one off a hillside volunteer and finished the race.

Down below, I spied a piece of green—a soccer field—lush and flat. Then, both suddenly and finally, I was there. Half mile to go, sprinting between a friendly gauntlet of spectators who bombarded us with cheers and claps. I tumbled in 12th, collapsed on Henning's back in the chute, then trudged off to find Diego for a massage.

A mustached veteran runner waited behind me, and he heard me mutter, "Never again," and meaning it, too.

"Don't ye have fell roonin' in the States, lad?" he said. Except for the fact that I understood him, I would have taken him for a Scotsman.

"Yeah, we have it," I said. "We call it hang gliding."

Day 3 Tuesday, July 25th
7-Mile Road Race
(Hyde)

"Now, here, you see, it takes all the running you can do, to keep in the same place." —Lewis Carrol, *Through the Looking Glass*

When recalling their races, British runners often talk about going through "a bad patch"—that time in the race when things look their bleakest. My struggle at the top of Hobson Moor on day two, for instance, was a classic "bad patch." But how long does a "bad patch" last? On the Tour, sometimes a whole race.

Day three proved to be my darkest hour on the Tour, and there was little solace in the knowledge that virtually everyone else felt just about as bad. "I won't kid you," Rob Taylor told me afterward, "my quads are absolutely shattered." To which I could only reply, "What quads?"

On the Tour, you're usually around the same group of racers each day. If, however, you begin to see runners you don't recognize from previous days, you're either racing better or *worse* than ever.

I saw a lot of new backs on day three. Runners zoomed by me, and it was like having one of those bad dreams where you run in place and get absolutely nowhere. My quads—pounded to smithereens on the slopes of the fell—ached with each downhill stride. I winced with every step. I had this twisted image stuck in my head: Yank in the RAF, coaxing his bullet-riddled Spitfire back to base for an emergency landing.

My base was Diego's massage table. I compounded my worst race (27th) of the Tour by failing to get right in line for a rub-down—more proof of a misfiring mind. By the time I flopped down on the table, the street lights were on in front of the Hyde Town Hall.

Day 4, Wednesday, July 26
Day Off

"The English never know when they are beaten." —Napoleon Bonaparte

Being in the Tour is kind of like being in a war. Every day you peek over the top of the trench and the war's still there. Every day you weigh your losses and how much ammunition you have left. Our day off arrived with all the fanfare of a one-day pass to some friendly village at the rear. But we'd be back at the front soon enough. The half-marathon (race four) hung over our heads like advance orders from the high command.

The temptation was to lounge around the hotel, alternating naps, hot whirlpools and megadoses of aspirin. Apparently, not everyone felt so beat up. Ultrarunner Eleanor Adams ran 20 miles on *her* day off.

What I did was bolt to nearby Wales, the theory being I needed to forget about the Tour, and riding through gray-stone villages with names I could neither spell nor pronounce might somehow help that. My wife drove, and I put the seat back and my blistered feet up on the dashboard. Then I limped up and down the steps of some ancient castle for a good part of the afternoon. Dinner was fish 'n' chips, wrapped in grease-soaked newspaper, in the car on the way back to Hyde.

Driving back, I couldn't help thinking about Billy from Buxton's warning that the Tour would be "bloody hell." I decided that running the Tour was only half the hell—*thinking* about each upcoming race was the other half. That's the problem with the day off, you've got too much time to think.

Dropping out was a thought, but not really an option. For one thing, it made way too much sense. But logic hasn't got a whole lot to do with the Tour. The Tour is about being British and keeping a "stiff upper lip." Besides, how would you tell a guy like Ron Hill—who's run every day (usually twice a day) for 25 years—that you can't finish his race because your legs are a wee bit sore? I'd have sooner done the Fell Run again than tell Hill I was bailing out. Listening to the hum of the rental car, I had a haunting vision of a bunch of British runners drinking ale at my favorite pub (Hare and Hounds, perched at the top of a Tameside heath), months later, talking about the American who cracked in the Tour. *Brit One (raised eyebrows):* "Chap clapped out on day three, I believe. Hmmmm. Bit of a soft lot, the Yanks." *Brit Two:* "Quite right, Nigel. Pity, really."

Day 5 Thursday, July 27
Half-Marathon
(Ashton-u-Lyne)

"There be some sports are painful, and their labour delight in them sets off."
—William Shakespeare, *The Tempest.*

Like a renewed barrage, it began again. We lined up for the half-marathon in the nearby town of Ashton-u-Lyne. Apparently regenerated from the day off, the leaders hammered through the opening miles. The two-loop course was relatively flat with a finish on the track. I lagged in the third or fourth cluster of runners, partly by design—a recommitment to my original "shark pack" strategy—and partly because I couldn't go any faster. For three miles, I felt like the un-oiled Tin Man, my stride all stiff and clanky. It took all my concentration just to stay with my own pack.

Then something happened that I really didn't count on: I gradually got "loose." It felt weird, and I didn't quite trust it to be true. I traded some pulls at the front of our pack. Other runners began to come back to us, and each catch seemed to fuel our advance. By five miles, we were sharks locked into a feeding-frenzy. Our group didn't break up until the final 5K.

I pounded onto the Richmond Street Athletic Track for the final 300 meters with one of the scrappy Stockport guys, John Holden, camped off my shoulder. A spectator on the infield leaned in and implored John, "Come on, stick 'em! Stick 'em!" And he did too, by two seconds, as I ran a 1:10:21 and placed 12th. Henning, my Danish friend, charged in a step behind me. Henning was taking an awful beating as the tour progressed, but his overall place was still well within the top ten—primarily on the strength of a sixth-place finish on the first day. The best race of the day went to the women's leader, Catherine Newman. She floated through a 1:12:47, good for 37th overall and a comfortable lead over the women's field.

From Ron Hill came good news. "Once you get through the half-marathon, it gets easier," he said. "You'll enjoy the last two days."

Enjoy? There were times when I was absolutely astounded by the sheer absurdity of it all. But damned if the Tour didn't radiate some old magic—the gladiator's simplistic glory in the ancient arena. It could suck you in. The Tour had a challenge and a cama-raderie you could cling to, and—once or twice—I caught myself thinking, "Next year, I'll *really* train for this." Then reality kicked in: "Nope. Never again, man. This is once and done."

Day 6 Friday, July 28
6.3-Mile Cross-Country Race
(Silver Springs, Ashton-u-Lyne)

"All I knew was that you had to run, run, run, without knowing why you were running . . . through fields that you didn't understand, and woods that made you afraid, over hills without knowing you'd been up and down. . . ." —Alan Sillitoe, *The Loneliness of the Long Distance Runner.*

Of course, there was still the cross-country race, and knowing Ron Hill, you could bet a few English pounds that the fifth stage wouldn't be any soft jaunt on the manicured fairways of the country club golf course.

Not to worry. Day six—the 6.3-mile cross-country race at Ashton-u-Lyne—was tailor-made for a groundhog. Sharp, little hills. Lots of ruts. A big ditch or two. A sideways duck through a small opening in a thick hedge. The course was, more or less, three roller-coaster loops over a dirt path. And, oh yeah, someone reminded me that Eddy broke a bone in his foot in this stage one year and had to drop out of the Tour. Great. Still, with the half-marathon behind us, our *esprit de corps* was high. Gathering for the start, the officials couldn't get us behind the line—not even close—and it took Hill himself to move us back: "If you move up any closer, lads, you'll be halfway to the bloody mile marker!"

We bolted off with extra incentive to get to the hedge opening before "rush hour." After the first mile, where I found myself racing alongside Petko Karpachev, a fast Bulgarian, I got scared and backed off, thinking I was out too fast. He'd been far ahead of me in all the previous stages. Later, of course, I'd wished I'd stuck with him, as Petko weaved his way up to 6th place on the bump-and-grind circuit.

I settled for 11th (35:05), which turned out to be my highest finish in any stage of the Tour. The debacle of my third race seemed in the distant past, and I knew I could muster one more racing effort.

By contrast, I felt badly for Henning, who, dragging a bad leg behind him, summoned all his strength to finish 35th in the fifth stage. The Tour could beat you up, and the Danish runner had the look of a boxer staving off a late-round knockout. Then again, a lot of us looked like that. After five races, looking at another pulverized runner, sore and sullen, was a lot like looking in the mirror.

Day 7, Saturday, July 29
9-Mile Canal Run
(Mossley to Hyde)

*"Ride on! Rough-shod if need be, smooth-shod if that will do,
but ride on! Ride on over all obstacles, and win the race!"* —Charles
Dickens

Before each stage of the Tour, race officials provided the results
of the previous day's race, plus the cumulative standings. So, going
into the final day, every runner knew where he or she stood. The
real question was who had what left. The final race began at two
p.m. at the top of Mossley village, where we would plunge down to
the canal and then run the narrow towpath back to the finish at
Hyde Town Square. This was the only day it rained. I watched Henning trot around the soccer field, trying to get loose as the English
rain came down in sheets. The Danish runner was clinging to ninth
place overall, and I knew he wanted desperately to hang on to top-
10 status. (He did, too, finishing ninth in the canal run and ninth
overall. "Viking blood," I told Henning. "That's how you did it.")

Me? I sat 13th overall, mimicking my bib number, more than
a half-minute behind 12th and about a minute ahead of 14th. Only
a dream race—or a totally disastrous one—could change my overall place.

By the time we hit the towpath, the rain had stopped, but the
footing was slick. I thought this race, at least, might be easy—like

training on the towpath along the Lehigh River back in Pennsylvania. But, no, the course had a Ron Hill twist to it: low bridges to duck under and cobblestone ramps to charge up that were as slippery as bars of bathtub soap.

The temptation was simply to run training pace. After all, a little voice reasoned, "Your overall place won't change. Why kill yourself?" But I put my head down, lifted stony legs and scratched and clawed for every second, every place. It seemed silly, but somehow I thought anything less than a racing effort would taint my performance—my Tour—and it didn't matter that I'd be the only one to realize it. In the middle, my shoe lace came loose, and I was irate about losing time when I stopped to tie it.

In the last mile, the sun broke out and the air grew hot and muggy along the waterway. We burst from behind a brick factory onto the road and began the final charge to the finish. I remember the sweet sting of sweat in my eyes, the tangy salt taste in my mouth and the crowd at Hyde Town Square cheering us in.

I finished 16th in the last stage, and 13th overall with a 4:48:19.

Rob Taylor, the veterans winner (by just 21 seconds over Tony Keller), sprinted in right after me, and when we came through the chute, he said: "Splendid Tour, Mark, splendid Tour!" Just him saying that meant a helluva lot more to me than the engraved finisher's medal—even though I liked the medal a lot.

I staggered around, half-dead, half-happy. Finishers everywhere shook hands, slapped backs, congratulated each other on finishing—fighting the Tour to a draw. You can't really *beat* the Tour of Tameside. The best you can hope for is to break even.

After

"We few, we happy few, we band of brothers. For he that sheds his blood with me today, shall be my brother." —William Shakespeare, *Henry VIII*

At the awards ceremony at Hyde Town Hall, Tour announcer Dickie Hughes had to calm everybody down a bit—especially the blokes in the balcony. "Keep your pints off the railing, lads. We don't want any accidents!" he pleaded.

Imagine that. You survive the Tour, then get bonked on the head by a falling pint of English stout.

Feeling festive, Eddy Hellebuyck passed around a magnum of champagne that looked to be at least half his size. He had a right to celebrate, too, making a clean sweep of six stages (4:25:35, total time), as did the women's winner Catherine Newman. Newman (5:05:46) set a new Tour of Tameside record, winning the women's division by almost 22 minutes.

In the middle of the celebration, a lady veteran from Stockport named Pauline Smith limped across the finish line. She'd ripped some knee ligaments in the cross-country race but wouldn't quit. Pauline had peg-legged it all the way down the canal towpath, her knee tightly wrapped, just to finish the Tour.

"I couldn't miss out on the champagne!" brimmed Pauline. Which is precisely the problem with these Brits, they never know when they're beaten.

Every year someone suggests that Ron Hill smooth out the Tour's rough spots. Take out the fell run. Cut down the distances.

Every year—for runners like Henning and me, Pauline Smith and Billy from Buxton—Hill refuses. The world doesn't need another flat, fast 5K. "The Tour isn't *supposed* to be easy," bristles Hill, who finished exactly 100th in the Tour despite a tender hamstring.

And amidst the clapping and cheering and clanking of pint glasses, I knew he was right. The struggle was "reason why" enough. It was that clear, that simple, and I felt a sudden sadness that the Tour was over, and worse, that I'd probably never be back.

Then the sadness was gone, flashing by like the stranger in my ear on top of Hobson Moor, his voice fading to the hiss of a whisper in the wind, "Come on, lad! Grind 'em out! Grind 'em out!"

AND THEN THE VULTURE EATS YOU

or

IN SEARCH OF THE GREAT BIG MYSTICAL UNBELIEVABLY IMPOSSIBLE KAHUNA

John L. Parker, Jr.

I was there when they invented running in America. It was on an undulating strip of road in Gainesville, Florida that Florida Track Club runners called "The Bacon Strip," otherwise known as Northwest 16th Avenue.

A group of us were training there in the early spring of 1970 when one of the guys, a wiry, dark-complected fellow from up North, announced: "I've been thinking about running a marathon."

Naturally, everyone counseled against it. For one thing, the marathon was a "road race," a distinctly pejorative term. We were "Track Men" and considered "road races" strictly local affairs, maybe good for a few grins and some easy trophies. For another, the event was ridiculously long. We were all milers, five and ten-thousand meter men. It wasn't that the distance itself was overly intimidating—most of us ran well in excess of 100 miles a week in training anyway—but we figured if you couldn't find out who was the better man after 6.2 miles of 400-meter laps, then the hell with it.

And marathoners seemed such a strange breed, even to us. Many affected facial hair and wire-rimmed glasses, some had Ph.D.s in arcane fields. And they all reveled in the obscurity of their event (a marathon in those days might have 30 or 40 people in it—sometimes fewer).

When a "marathoner" occasionally ventured onto the track, he was nonchalantly drawn and quartered.

But here was the part that befuddled us. Marathoners didn't care if you beat them! They seemed almost proud of the fact that they weren't very fast. Their knowing smiles and ethereal comments implied a mystical wisdom that could only be won in that granddaddy, that king, that ultimate of all long-distance challenges. Oh, we could win our little races and have our fun, but we could never know True Enlightenment until we had personally experienced the Great Big Mystical Unbelievably Impossible Kahuna.

We didn't buy that crap, and on that spring day in 1970 we couldn't believe our friend was buying it.

"Hey, you don't want to run the marathon, man," someone said.

"Marathoners wear *hats*," I said. "So what if you *could* win one of the things. Who cares? You're a Track Man. The track's where the action is. That's where the important events are run. Plus, it's a good life. You get invited to the big meets, you get to keep the soap and the stationery from the motel. You don't want to run the marathon . . . *Frank.*"

Well, Frank Shorter did want to run the marathon and shortly after he won the gold medal in Munich in 1972 that proud, exclusive little band of Mystic Marathoners was shocked and horrified to find that Bob, Joe, Buddy, Sis, and old Grandma herself were all reading articles on carbohydrate-loading and trying to figure out what kind of splits they would have to hit next Saturday to qualify for Boston.

Races where you used to personally know every single soul now had entrants in the thousands. And they were walking around afterwards, sipping beer and grinning these big, oh, I don't know, *grins*.

Not only that, but more and more track men such as Shorter were moving up from 10,000 meters, and guess what? They were *fast*. These guys were hitting five minutes a mile and better, and they weren't talking Enlightenment and Knowledge, they were talking Prize Money.

Wait a minute! Hold on just a second here! Time out! The Executive Committee of the Mystical Marathoners has just convened and decided that the marathon is no longer where it's at. No. Not at all. Sorry for all the bother. Henceforth, anyone wishing to achieve the Great Big Mystical Unbelievably Impossibly Kahuna will have to participate in an *ultra* event.

What's an Ultra event?

Well, it's any Great Big Impossible Race that's either longer than a marathon—50 miles will do, 100 is better—or that has a marathon as just one of its components.

Hence your Western States 100. Hence your Ironman

Triathlon. Hence your, God help us, Ultimate Runner.

But because Track Men don't run 100-milers and Mystic Marathoners sink like rocks in water, it is in this cruelly-conceived Ultimate Runner event where the clash between the two groups continues in its purest form even to this day, each side wreaking havoc, humiliation, and occasionally permanent soft-tissue injury on the other. In this unique five-race event the playing field seems almost level for the first time: Every stripe of runner is practically guaranteed to be staggering by the end. Both the Track Men and the Mystic Ultras seem to more or less enjoy the carnage. What more could you ask of a weekend?

୧◆

Every November, Jackson, MI, an hour's drive west of Detroit, lays claim to hosting a Great Big You-Know-What. It's not the longest, or the most exotic, but it's certainly one of the more imaginative of the lot.

Picture this. You start off bright and early Saturday morning with a brisk 10,000-meter road race. Nothing unusual so far, right? Okay, but then you walk around for a few minutes and catch your breath, and head for the track. That's right, the track.

There you race, in fairly rapid succession, a 400-meters, a 100-meters, and a mile. Then at two o'clock in the afternoon, you line up on the road in front of Jackson Community College and you cap off your day by running a marathon. Twenty-six-point-two miles through the quiet streets of Jackson.

You are awarded points in each of the five races based strictly on your time. The most points at the end of the day wins. Of course, there's a catch: You've got to *finish* all the events for your score to count.

The point table is a purely mathematical extrapolation based on the current world records in each event, with a world record worth the maximum of 1,200 points. What's so devilish is that the 100-yard dash is worth as many points as the marathon, so no one can really afford to sandbag in any event. You've got to try at or near your best in every event or fall hopelessly behind.

As an example of how the scoring works, times of 10.14 in the 100 meters, 46:02 in the 400, 3:59 in the mile, 28:40 in the 10K, and 2:16:14 in the marathon, are all worth the same number of points: 1,000. No one has ever achieved any of those times, by the way. The winning total is usually in the area of 2,000 points for all five events.

The attraction to both the Track Men and the Mystic Ultras is immediately obvious. Both types would rather win a race by mental scheming or trickery than by sheer ability, so it is the perfect intellectual—as well as physical—challenge. A Track Man would look at the schedule and say: "Hmmm. All right, three out of the five events are almost sheer speed events. My God, the Ultras'll make fools of themselves out there. A respectable 10K is well within my grasp. Sooo, the thing to do is to hold my own in the 10K, burn the track events, and then survive the marathon. Piece of cake."

A Mystic Ultra would look at the same schedule and say: "Wow. Three out of the five events are almost sheer speed events. But how far ahead of you can someone get in a 100-yard dash? So you give up a little ground, so what? On the other hand, a decent marathon at the end of a day of racing would be nearly an impossible feat for most runners, but any Mystic Ultra would just be getting warmed up. A respectable 10K is well within my grasp. Sooo, the thing to do is to hold my own in the 10K, cruise through the track events with as much dignity as possible, and then blast the marathon, leaving the Track Men scattered like carrion on the roads of Jackson. Piece of cake."

The funny thing about it is that both sides are right. And while over the years the Track Men have claimed most of the top finishes and the lion's share of the prize money ($3,750 each for first open man and woman), the Mystic Ultras have at least had the satisfaction of witnessing some of the more spectacular Track Man explosions ever recorded in the annals of foot racing. If The Ultimate Runner is fiendish in its conception, it is only a point of great pride to Mike McGlynn, an elfin and generally unassuming associate professor of Health and Fitness at Jackson Community College, who founded the event in 1983 with author and fitness consultant Charlie Kuntzleman.

"It just came to us one day while we were running," said McGlynn. "We were trying to come up with something, uh, different."

That first year 22 people finished this different event and McGlynn was immensely relieved to find that no one had actually died. He figured it just might go big time. Oh, it could never be the kind of gigantic spectacle many road races had become. The logistics were too formidable for that. Each competitor, for instance, is furnished a "personal jogger" whose job it is to fetch things and otherwise serve as batman for his liege. Mounds of food are provided during the day. Cots are set up in a special area in the gym to allow for rest between events.

As a matter of fact, after about the third heat in the mile, when the Mystic Ultras are wandering in, stiff-legged from the short events, and the Track People are lying around in various stages of hypoglycemia, the whole shebang in the gym begins to resemble nothing so much as a World War I field hospital after some real unpleasantness in the trenches.

On the other hand, the self-limiting nature of the event had a certain appeal. Wasn't a certain exclusivity in fact part of what the Mystic Ultras were looking for in the first place, back before everybody and his accountant starting running marathons, fer crissakes, back before you had to run 50Ks and 100Ks and 100-milers just to get away from the rabble? And so by 1986 a full house of 100 runners had signed up. The Ultimate Runner, it seems, was being talked up among the Mystic Ultras, and a prize money structure was attracting enough talented Track Men to make it interesting. And there was this: If you listened carefully to the chatter you could overhear people saying things like "Just Finishing Is Winning" and "You're Not Running Against Other People, You're Running Against Yourself" and "The Goal is Not to Win, the Goal is to Transcend," and such. McGlynn and his partner must have known at that moment that they had done it. He and Charlie Kuntzleman had created a Great Big Mystical Unbelievably Impossible Kahuna.

ॐ

The Ultimate Runner of 1988, although without prize money for the first time in several years and thus missing some top past Track Men and Mystic Ultras, nonetheless offered many of the features and much of the madness that made the event just so darned much fun. First, the weather was crazy, starting in the 70's, humid as a greenhouse, ending with a chilly drizzle slowly turning everyone into blue-gray blobs of protoplasm in the marathon. Missing were Track Man Roger Soler, the business-like Peruvian Olympian who had won top money the past two years, as well as internationally known Mystic Ultras Charlie Trayer and Barney Klecker.

Nonetheless, the contest was still a clash between the two groups, although the hauteur and inexperience of the Track Men this year was beyond anything witnessed in the past. First there was Peter Churney, who showed up at the pre-race banquet the night before resplendent in suit, suspenders and floral-patterned tie. The tall, strong, good-looking 30-year-old Californian was perfect for the part: He was a four-minute miler from central casting. He is also the only human being to ever confess that his life's ambition is to be a TV weatherman.

"I'm in pretty good shape," Churney allowed. "Not the best I've ever been in, but pretty good. I think I'll do all right."

The implication was that old Pete thought he would do a whole lot better than "all right." In fact, he had flown his mother in from Rhode Island to watch Petey do his thing. But there was this: Peter Churney had never in his life run a marathon. Ever. And there he was in his suspenders, sipping beer, and talking "all right." Typical Track Man.

Then there was Ed Cosme, a tough 28-year-old fireplug of a

Track Man from Brooklyn who had run a marathon, albeit only in 2:55. But he listed personal bests of sub-4:30 in the mile, sub-13 in the 100, sub-54 400, and sub 32 in the 10K. He was no pushover and he was in good shape.

The Track Man nobody could figure was soft-spoken 25-year-old Canadian student George Kepenyes. Gangly, pale, Kepenyes was a real speedster: He had run 48 seconds for 400 meters, and 1:47 for 800. Surely anyone that fast would be a candidate for a mid-marathon body bag. But George claimed a 2:48 26-miler on his resumé.

You can always tell the Mystic Ultras on the Ultimate Runner program where the competitors list their best times. Most runners stop at the marathon. The Mystic Ultras keep right on listing. Steve Webster, a 34-year-old from Holland, Michigan, had a 4:11 38-mile ultra to his credit. His 2:43 marathon was certainly respectable, and his sprint times, at least for a Mystic Ultra, were not entirely laughable. He had finished ninth the previous year and he was back in excellent shape. With the Track Men such unknown quantities, would this be the year of the Mystic Ultra, and would Steve Webster be the one to finally bring home the banner?

The only other Mystic Ultra in contention was 27-year-old Mark Elderbrock, who had finished 12th in 1987. He listed a 31:50 10K, so-so track times, and a 2:34 marathon. He listed no ultra times, but there was this note appended to his entry: ". . . has finished the Hawaiian Ironman three times." He was a Mystic Ultra, all right.

On race morning, despite the mugginess, Churney poured it on in the 10K and his 32:56 made him the man to beat with 468 points. Cosme's 33:25 left him less than 30 points back, and Kepenyes's 34:24 brought him in third. Veterans Elderbrock and Webster laid way off the pace and wound up in 12th and 13th place with 34:55 and 36:17, respectively.

Churney wandered around the field hospital, confused-looking, soaking wet, his entire body flushed red as a beet. "I don't know what the matter is," he said, looking down at himself.

"You're sweating, man," someone offered helpfully.

Then it was over to the track for the day's first round of comic relief, courtesy of the Mystic You-Know-Who's. In this regard Charlie Trayer was much missed. In 1986 writer/runner Don Kardong wrote that Trayer looked like a cross between a leprechaun and Yosemite Sam. And if you've never had yourself a good belly laugh at the expense of another athlete, you should watch a Yosemite Sam lookalike sprinting a full-out quarter-mile in 64.4 seconds without so much as bending a knee. But Trayer is far from alone. All the M.U.'s can be identified on the track by a single distinguishing feature: Their form and pace look exactly the same whether they're running a marathon or a 100-meter dash. The only way you can tell they're sprinting is the fire in their eyes.

Oh, the Track Men try not be so crass as to actually laugh out loud, but you can tell it's not easy. Even the Mystic Ultras have to admit it's pretty amusing. And besides, they know who gets the last laugh: The Vulture.

Kardong also came up with The Vulture. Don was fourth in the 1976 Olympic marathon, but his real claim to fame is a fifth in the 1986 Ultimate Runner. Afterwards he said: "The marathon is a like a vulture sitting on your shoulder during all the other events.

And then at the end of the day, the vulture eats you."

It was that same year that Jeff Galloway, a former Florida Track Clubber and Olympian, bailed out of the event sometime during the marathon. He told the press: "I haven't had so much fun since Vietnam!"

Strangely enough, the first track event, the 400-meters, turned out to be the decisive race in the 1988 Ultimate Runner. Half-miler George Kepenyes blasted a 51.3 to catapult him to a 75-point lead over Churney, who managed a 55.6. Cosme was 30 points back with a 55.7. Elderbrock and Webster did okay considering the aforementioned knee problem of all Mystic Ultras, hitting 63.1 and 60.4, but they were way back in 11th and 13th places, biding their time.

Kepenyes's 12.1 100 padded his lead to nearly 150 points over Cosme (12.5) and Churney (13.4). By running in the mid-14's Elderbrock dropped to 12th and Webster hung on to 13th. Churney grimly fought his way back into second with his 4:34 mile, but Kepenyes (4:47) would still be nearly 100 points ahead going into the marathon, and Cosme (4:44) was only 30 points behind Churney. With 5:06 and 5:02, Elderbrock and Webster hung grimly onto 12th and 13th, but by this time they were nearly 430 points out of first. Their only hope was to bring in superlative marathon times and hope that the Track Men found more Enlightenment than usual in the final event.

As expected, the marathon featured a veritable firecracker string of Exploding Track Men. Kepenyes, riding his 100-point lead for all it was worth, started off slow and then tapered off.

Uncharacteristically for a Track Man, he was approaching the event gingerly. Cosme tried to steal the whole show, building up a four-minute lead by the 16-mile mark. Shortly thereafter he was seen on the side of the road. His personal jogger had abandoned his bicycle and was pounding on Cosme's quadriceps like a kettle drummer for the New York Philharmonic. Now it was Churney's turn. At the 18-mile mark he had assumed a commanding lead. At the 18.3-mile mark, he had assumed the hands-on-knees fetal death grip and was begging someone, anyone, for Gatorade. Kepenyes might have found the sight mildly comforting, but he was several miles back, operating at what might best be described as a moderately brisk stroll. Churney, as he struggled along at something like a crab-walk himself, heard about Kepenyes's problems and suddenly brightened: "I can still win this sucker!" Webster took over the lead, plotting, at long last, Mystic Ultra revenge. But even *he* was in for a surprise. Kepenyes and Churney somehow managed to finish in 3:20 and 3:17, but their form looked more like something you would see at a county fair three-legged race. Kepenyes's conservative strategy, however, paid off: He won the overall event. Churney ended up third. Cosme, the tough New Yorker, despite his recalcitrant thighs, ran a 3:07 to edge out Churney for second place, only 72 points behind Kepenyes.

Webster and Elderbrock finished first and second in the men's division of the marathon in 2:57 and 2:58, not enough to move them up in the standings. They placed 13th and 12th overall, behind a veritable gaggle of Track Men. Perhaps they took some small comfort from the sight of Churney in the field hospital, shaken and pale as a ghost, huddled under a space blanket, gulping any manner of liquid handed to him. The next day he was heard to say: "I can't believe I was such an arrogant ass."

The overall winner of the marathon portion of the event was neither a Track Man nor a Mystic Ultra. The winner was Ella Willis, who passed Webster shortly after 21 miles and never looked back, cruising in serenely to beat all comers in the last event in 2:55:31. She also won *all* the other women's events.

Well known in Detroit running circles, Ella is the kind of competitor who might do the Ultimate Runner on Saturday, a road race on Sunday, and a marathon the following weekend. In fact, in 1985 she did just that, finishing second in the Detroit marathon and winning the other two races.

Until 1987 Ella had not only won every Ultimate Runner women's contest, she had won every women's *event* in every Ultimate Runner. Neither a Mystic Ultra nor a Track Woman, Ella is what you might call a Maniac Runner, and a Maniac Runner who is not currently hospitalized or on crutches is a formidable adversary. If you're a female with designs on Ultimate Runner glory you don't have a vulture on your shoulder, you have Ella.

ઠ્વ

The 1987 Ultimate Runner, which offered prize money, was noteworthy in two other respects. It featured the closest, hardest-fought confrontation to date between the Track Men and Mystic Ultras, and it also featured possibly the most pyrotechnical implosion of a Track Man yet recorded. It made Churney's 1988 devastation look like a mild lack of concentration.

To start off the chilly, blustery day, five of the Track Men ran around 31 minutes or better in the 10K, good for about 600 points, with 1986 winner Roger Soler, a Peruvian Olympic team member, edged out by a 37-year-old former University of Kentucky star Paul Baldwin in an event record, 30:31 to 30:40. Baldwin's all-out sprint to win the 10K raised many eyebrows. Was he really that good, or had no one clued him in?

About 100 points back were Mystic Ultra stars Barnie Klecker and Charlie Trayer, who cruised in with 32:48 and 33:15. In keeping with tradition, neither Klecker or Trayer looked much like runners. Klecker, a lanky Minnesotan renowned for 50- and 100-mile events, looks more like a middle linebacker. And the aforementioned Trayer has already been associated with the appropriate cartoon character.

The veteran Soler methodically built up his lead on the track, running a second place 12.8 in the 100, and a winning 4:25.5 mile. But although he would be several hundred points ahead going into the marathon, Baldwin and three other Track Men were still in contention. And naturally, both Trayer and Klecker, flaunting the true M.U. attitude that Kardong's vulture was a sort of house pet, figured that when the marathon rolled around it was Anything Can Happen Time in Glycogen Depletion Land.

Well, what happened was the Great Track Man Explosion of 1987. It turned out that Paul Baldwin, who had sprinted to set the 10K record that very morning, was one of those Track Men who entered the Ultimate Runner without ever having run a marathon in his life. Ever. But that did not stop him from bolting into the lead, in true Track Man style, at the 18-mile mark and attempting to run away not only from the conservatively paced Soler, but also from leaders Klecker and Trayer.

And Baldwin was in fact several minutes ahead at the 23-mile mark, where he veered off the course and more or less just sort of crashed into a drainage ditch.

"All I remember is passing the 23-mile marker and then lying flat on my back looking up at people all around me," he said later from a hospital bed. His body temperature at the emergency room was 94, leading to speculation that it had been around 90 out there in the old ditch. They kept him for a couple of days, treating him for low blood sugar, hypothermia, and lack of sleep. It seems he had pulled a late shift at his job the night before arriving, and hadn't slept at all in the previous 24 hours.

Trayer ran in powerfully to win the marathon in 2:36, followed by Klecker in 2:42—impressive but only good enough for fifth and sixth overall. Once again the Track Men won most of the goodies. Soler cruised in with a solid 2:48, finishing fourth in the marathon but first overall, netting $4,050 in prize money. Trayer earned $400 and Klecker $200. But more importantly, they won the kind of True Enlightenment a Mystic Ultra experiences when he watches a haughty Track Man cashing in his chips at the Last Gasp Saloon within veritable spitting distance of the finish line.

And there are some things in this world money just can't buy.

About the Writers

James E. Shapiro is the author of *Ultramarathon* and *Meditations From the Breakdown Lane*. A veteran of many ultras and shorter races, he is now a schoolteacher in New York City.

Don Kardong is the author of *Thirty Phone Booths to Boston*. A frequent contributor to *Runner's World* and other magazines, he was also director of the Association of Road Racing Athletes. Mr. Kardong was fourth in the 1976 Olympic marathon in Montreal. He lives in Spokane.

Kenny Moore, author of *Best Efforts*, was a senior writer for *Sports Illustrated*. A champion collegiate athlete at the University of Oregon, Mr. Moore was fourth in the 1972 Olympic marathon in Munich. He lives in Kailua, Hawaii.

Hal Higdon is the author of *On the Run from Dogs and People*, *The Masters Running Guide*, *The Marathoners*, and 21 other books. He is a senior writer for *Runner's World* and contributes to many other magazines. Mr. Higdon is the first runner to win national titles at the junior, open and masters level. He lives in Michigan City, Indiana.

Ed Ayres, author of *What's Good for GM*, is the founder and for many years the editor of *Running Times*. A long-time competitor in ultras and other races, he lives in Washington, DC.

Tom Hart, a former editor at Houghton Mifflin Company and a former literary agent, is now a retired English teacher in the Boston area. He has contributed to *The Runner* and other magazines. He is a veteran marathoner with several sub-three hour efforts to his credit.

Mark Will-Weber is a former editor and writer at *Runner's World* and coaches track and cross country at Moravian College. He was an All-IC4A cross country runner in college and has run a marathon in 2:22:30. He lives in Bethlehem, Pennsylvania.

John L. Parker, Jr. is the author of the novels *Once a Runner* and *Again to Carthage* as well as *Runners & Other Dreamers, Heart Monitor Training for the Compleat Idiot,* and several other books. He was editorial director of *Running Times* magazine and has contributed to *Outside, Runner's World, Ultrasport,* and other magazines. He was the Southeastern Conference mile champion three times, as well as the national USTFF steeplechase champion and three-mile runnerup. He lives in Bar Harbor, Maine and Gainesville, Florida.